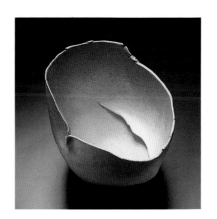

GREAT POTS

CONTEMPORARY CERAMICS

FROM FUNCTION TO FANTASY

GREAT POTS

CONTEMPORARY CERAMICS
FROM FUNCTION TO FANTASY

ULYSSES GRANT DIETZ

THE NEWARK MUSEUM
Newark, New Jersey

GUILD Publishing
Madison, Wisconsin

Jacket front: Elsa Rady, *En Deco,* 1986; see page 90.

Jacket back: (clockwise from top left): Rondina Huma, jar with painted decoration, 1979; see page 64. Brother Thomas (Thomas Bezanson), bottle vase, 1975; see page 168. Babs Haenen, *Iced Stem Cup,* 1994; see page 173. Albert Green, square bottle vase, 1989; see page 47. Ron Nagle, *Vermilion to One,* 2000; see page 192. Phillip Maberry, urn on plinth, 1990; see page 189.

Endpaper front: Toshiko Takaezu, plate, 1971; see page 205.

Endpaper back: Henry Varnum Poor, bowl with design of wild turkeys, 1948; see page 50.

Page 1: Richard DeVore, *Vessel with Interior Shelf, #1027,* 2001; see page 85.

Page 3: Richard Kjaergaard, teapot with tooled surface, 1955; see page 131.

Opposite: fig. 1. Kenneth Ferguson, *Black Basket with Three Hares,* 1986. Thrown and handbuilt stoneware. Purchase 1987 Harry E. Sautter Bequest Fund (87.106). Purchased from the Garth Clark Gallery, New York City. 14.75"H x 16.5"W x 13.5"D.

Page 6: fig. 2. Piet Stockmans, *Object with Box,* 1998. Porcelain, wood. Gift of Garth Clark and Mark Del Vecchio, 2001 (2001.78.6.1-12a, b). 0.75"H x 17"Dia (largest dish).

Great Pots
Contemporary Ceramics from Function to Fantasy
Ulysses Grant Dietz

Published by GUILD Publishing
An imprint of GUILD, LLC
931 E. Main Street
Madison, Wisconsin 53703
TEL 608-257-2590
FAX 608-257-2690

Design: Laura Lindgren
Editor: Katie Kazan
Photography: Richard Goodbody, except pages 12, 15, 16 and 18: Noel Allum

A project of The Newark Museum
49 Washington Street
Newark, New Jersey 07102
TEL 973-596-6550

Distributed by North Light Books
An imprint of F&W Publications, Inc.
4700 East Galbraith Road
Cincinnati, Ohio 45236
TEL 800-289-0963

Copyright © 2003 The Newark Museum Association

ISBN (hardcover) 1-893164-18-7
ISBN (softcover) 1-893164-19-5

Printed in China

This book is published in conjunction with the exhibition *Great Pots: Contemporary Ceramics from Function to Fantasy* at The Newark Museum, February 14–June 1, 2003. Publication was made possible by a grant from the Friends of Contemporary Ceramics.

The Newark Museum, a not-for-profit museum of art, science and education, receives operating support from the City of Newark, the State of New Jersey, the New Jersey State Council on the Arts/Department of State, and corporate, foundation and individual donors. Funds for acquisitions and activities other than operations are provided by members and other contributors.

CONTENTS

FOREWORD

Great Pots is, historically, the sequel to *The Newark Museum Collection of American Art Pottery.* That volume, which was also written by Ulysses Grant Dietz, was published in 1984 for the Museum's seventy-fifth anniversary. Just as it was the first publication of The Newark Museum's important collection of American art pottery spanning the 1880s to the 1920s, *Great Pots* is the first to document Newark's holdings in studio ceramics, making this book yet another landmark in our institution's history.

Connoisseurship, the skill by which objects are categorized into realms of "good, better and best," is often considered the sole foundation from which art museums acquire and present their collections. Curators are initially trained as connoisseurs; the success of their training is manifested in their exhibitions and collections. However, such ranking has an invidious side effect, for it tends to minimize the inherent cultural value, as well as the inherent craft quality or aesthetic interest, of objects not necessarily deemed masterpieces.

From its founding in 1909, The Newark Museum has intentionally collected objects traditionally viewed as typical, even ordinary. Masterpieces were also collected, but—especially in the decorative arts—it was understood that masterpieces are far removed from the reality of most people and that typical, often common, examples of material culture can more eloquently express the way in which objects and everyday life interact in human culture. This collecting philosophy, which continues to the present day, is in part the heritage of John

PETER VOULKOS
LOS ANGELES, CA

Plate, 1981. Thrown and altered stoneware. See page 177.

9

Cotton Dana, Newark's founding director. Dana criticized the fetishization of masterpieces by major art museums at the turn of the century and desired to reach out to the average citizen.

This desire was seen in the Museum's early (1909, 1910 and 1912) exhibitions of modern and applied arts at a time when no other American museum considered these categories worthy of exhibition. Its most radical expression was a series of 1929 exhibitions, completed just after Dana's death, of hundreds of objects purchased for 10 cents, 50 cents and $1 at regional stores. Dana envisioned these shows in part to prove his adage that "Beauty has no relation to age, rarity or price." A beautiful object that is beyond the reach of the viewer has less transformative power than a beautiful object that he or she could actually purchase and have in his or her own home, or so the theory went.

When the Museum's associate director, Mildred Baker, purchased studio ceramics in 1949; when the first curator of decorative arts, Margaret White, was collecting studio pottery in the 1950s; and when J. Stewart Johnson was collecting ceramics in London in the mid-1960s, each sought *decorative arts* objects that could be interpreted as part of a domestic, rather than a museum, context. While of course interested in the artistic merit of the pieces they acquired for the Museum, they were unconcerned as to whether or not the pieces were "art." Instead, they asked: were they good pots? Did they show the maker's skill at handling clay, glazes, decoration? If they were functional, did they work?

The Newark Museum's interdepartmental ceramic holdings number thousands of objects and embrace human culture across the world, from prehistory to the present. Newark's collection of studio vessels of the post-Depression era—like the museum's holdings of art pottery from 1880 to 1930—have become part of the larger pantheon of ceramic history. The museum continues a distinguished heritage of collecting ceramics with an eye to developing a broadly brushed, but nonetheless vivid, picture of the importance of the ceramic vessel in the course of history.

Once again, Ulysses Dietz has brought his commanding knowledge to a project, for which we are deeply grateful. The Trustees of The Newark Museum and I also express our great appreciation to Linda Leonard Schlenger and the Friends of Contemporary Ceramics for encouragement of the highest order.

Mary Sue Sweeney Price, Director

August 2002

3
RALPH BACERRA
LOS ANGELES, CA

Plate with Japanesque design, 1976. Thrown porcelain with enamels. Purchase 1991 Louis Bamberger Bequest Fund (91.8). Purchased from the Garth Clark Gallery, New York City. 2"H x 13.5"Dia.

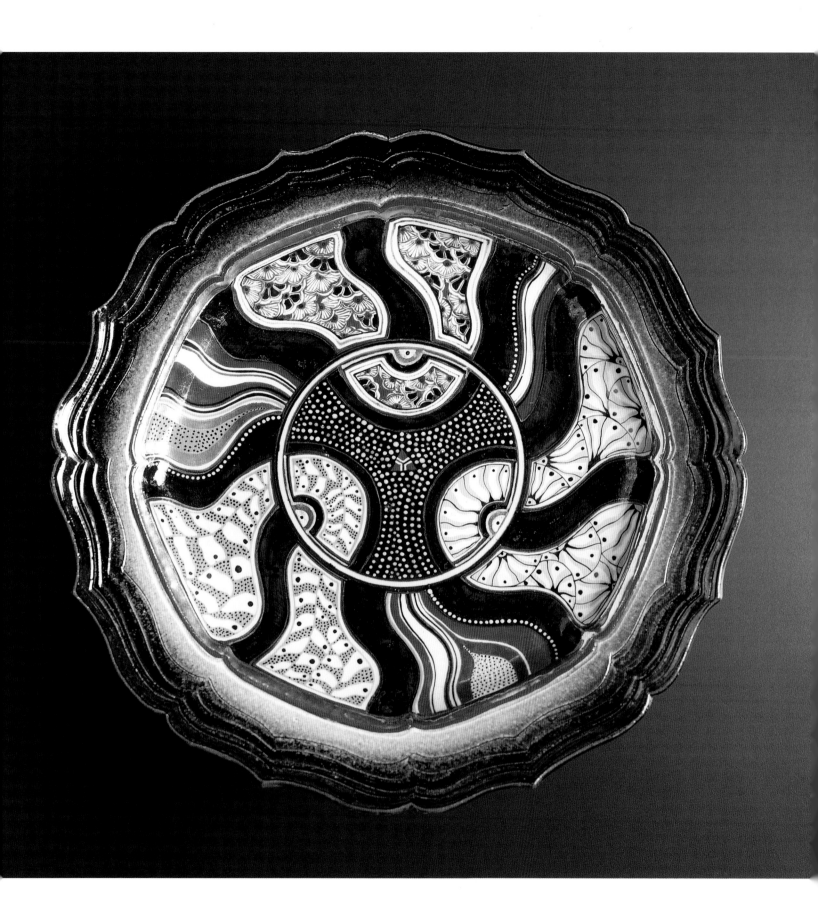

REMARKS ON POT MADNESS

GARTH CLARK AND MARK DEL VECCHIO

4

PETER VOULKOS
LOS ANGELES, CA

Stack Pot, *1975–82. Wood-fired stoneware. 39.5"H x 12"Dia.*

Michael Cardew, the doyen of the functional pottery world, referred to man's inexplicable passion for the humble pot as "pot madness," a kind of aesthetic dementia that fills one's mind with the desire to acquire hollow ceramic forms. We are not speaking of the mild version of this malady, finding a few vases at a swap meet or garage sale to decorate the kitchen, but the heavy-duty variety. It is an obsessive pursuit, like all serious collecting, that defies the limits of logic, domestic space and income. We have no idea just how long it has been part of civilization but we do know that it afflicted Chinese emperors before the birth of Christ, that shoguns waged wars to capture renowned potters and that European kings in the seventeenth and eighteenth centuries traded their royal guards for rare Chinese porcelains.

Some in the fine arts suggest that this pursuit made sense in the past, when art options were fewer. But in a contemporary landscape caught up in the electronic embrace of virtual reality, the purists argue that pots are now anachronisms. Yet the opposite is true. Pot collecting has grown into a gigantic activity from the most populist of the industrial-made decorative arts to the most rarefied of ancient treasures.

Indeed, one finds a particularly large and passionate group of pot collectors within the contemporary fine arts itself. We personally know at least a dozen major pot collectors among the world's leading art dealers, and a slew of major artists besides: Jasper Johns, Gilbert and George and Ellsworth Kelly, to name but a few. Andy Warhol, Robert Mapplethorpe and Dan Flavin are others from our recent past who also succumbed totally to the vessel's voluptuous and volumetric charm.

For these and other collectors of contemporary studio ceramics—including ourselves—the mere possession of a pot is not the thrill. Indeed, the joy comes later, once the pot has found a place in our home and has begun its dialogue not just with us but also with the other pots in the collection. It's what pots "do" and "say" that make them interesting. To this end, we offer some examples.

Service for Eight (ca. 1982–92) was made for us by Beatrice Wood, the Mama of Dada and the Queen of Luster Pottery. Much like the potter herself, this service comes with impeccable art credentials. *Art in America* declared it "one of the great uncontested masterpieces of late-twentieth-century American contemporary art." When that announcement was made, Mark decided that we should stop using it, but we still do, though less often. Beatrice made the service for us over a period of ten years, with each new addition to the service arriving as our Christmas gift, usually with a note of apology for these "awful, poorly made pots." Beatrice had dinner on the service in 1993 when she was in New York to be honored by the American Craft Council on the occasion of her one-hundredth birthday (she lived to 105). Toward the end of the meal she cast a critical eye over our dinner table and her dishes and admitted, "You know, they aren't half bad."

Those new to ceramics may be confused. Are we talking about dining on these plates, and yet also calling them "art"? If you are a fine arts fundamentalist, you probably have Kasimir Malevich's dictum ringing in your ears: "If it's useful it cannot be art." We would rather follow the wisdom of Wood's lover and mentor Marcel Duchamp, who told Beatrice, "There are no rules in art."

The service comprises more than 60 pieces. It is glazed in various lusters ranging from dusty pink-golds, viridians and peacock blues to shiny coppers shot with turquoise and streaked with pewter. Assembled on a table it generates an overwhelming sense of opulence, a dazzling show of refracted light. Furthermore this show is neither fixed nor static. Luster reflects the changing temperature and light over the course of a day; tonalities shift from, say, an undertow of green and gold in the morning to pink, mauve and silver in the later afternoon. Each glaze responds differently, and the combined impact of scores of iridescent

5
BEATRICE WOOD
OJAI, CA

Place setting from Service for Eight, *ca. 1982–92. Earthenware with luster glazes. 4"–9"H.*

objects on one surface, perpetually shifting color, mood and tonality, is positively psychedelic.

In contrast to the preciousness of the surfaces, Wood's forms are archaic and rudimentary, informally thrown with the artist's telltale "wobbly" throwing lines, a perfect and unpretentious foil to the over-the-top extravagance of the glazes. This work lives almost entirely in the realm of the nonliteral left brain; Wood has not inserted any asides to historical style, no message, metaphors or symbols. Her dinner service is irony-free and unapologetically hedonistic. It surrenders itself completely to the celebration of beauty, life and sensuality.

Our familiarity with the forms and functions of pots is part of what makes them accessible as art. Thus we can enter the aesthetic experience with more confidence than when faced with some of the arts' more esoteric explorations, which seem designed somehow to alienate.

Beatrice made her annual gift subject to the requirement that we use the service, and periodically she would check to see that we were honoring our commitment. She knew that however ravishing this service might be on display, it would be even more impressive in use. She was right, of course. When used, the service becomes four-dimensional, with the added immediacy and transcendence of art meeting life.

Is it art? We believe so, but either way this is an experience the worlds of photography, print, painting and video simply cannot deliver, an impotence that is, perhaps, the root cause of their advocates' frequent rejection of the functional as "nonart." By the late sixteenth century, the Japanese had embraced functional art through objects of exceptional visual power employed in the Zen tea ceremony; this refined, stylized choreography of the mind and senses still trumps most present-day performance art.

Another cherished functional work, a Gwari casserole, is one of two nearly identical pieces made by Michael Cardew in 1972. One was for Garth and the other for the Smithsonian Institution. In one sense, the casserole is more complicated than Wood's service. While it contains much of the same utilitarian joyfulness (minus the hedonism, as it is made by a British potter), it is also loaded with cross-cultural information that extends its aesthetic impact way beyond its function as a casserole. In other words, we are now getting into intriguing, amplifying, footnotes.

Cardew, one of the great potters of the twentieth century, remains a godlike figure among those who make functional wares. Cardew's career is divided into two parts. The English period lasted from 1921, when he joined Bernard Leach as his first Western apprentice, to 1939. During this time Cardew made pots that

6
MICHAEL CARDEW
WENFORD BRIDGE, ENGLAND

Gwari casserole, 1972.
Stoneware, temmoku glaze.
8"H x 11.5"Dia.

were inspired by the traditional English slipwares of the preindustrial era. However, it was in Africa—he worked in the Gold Coast (now Ghana) from 1942 to 1948 and in Abuja, Nigeria, from 1950 to 1965—that he produced his most expressive work, creating pieces that the Victoria and Albert Museum's Winfield Digby called "amongst the most beautiful [stoneware] to come from the hands of any modern potter."

The shape of this casserole is taken from the traditional pit-fired cooking pot made by the Gwari people near Abuja, where Cardew ran a small pottery school and workshop. He sought to capture the innate spirit of the locally produced vessels, while modifying their shape for contemporary usage. His pot was given a flat foot so that it could stand firmly, and he eventually adjusted the traditional three-handled form. The traditional pots were designed to be slung over a fire; Cardew's would be pulled from a modern oven, and two handles made extrication easier and safer.

Cardew also changed the Gwari lid. When we asked him why he chose to shift from the original concave lid to a convex one, he at first seemed puzzled by the question, then he scratched his chin (something he did whenever facing a vexing question) and said, "I think it is because there is something religious about a dome shape." While not a religious man, Cardew wanted this cooking vessel to signify ritual, and what symbolizes ritual more eloquently in the West than the dome of a cathedral?

The decoration is vaguely African although not all that different from the elemental slip decoration Cardew applied so dexterously in prewar Britain. The glaze on the African pots was made from local materials that Cardew unearthed in abandoned mines and other sources. They were unique in their character, still raw and unpredictable, speckled with impurities and melded by the fire into fine, satin textures.

To the very end of his career, Cardew made only pots that had a functional purpose, and despite his celebrity he priced them modestly to encourage use. In respect of this (and because it cooks so well), our Gwari casserole remains in active service.

Parisienne Chainsaw Massacre (fig. 7) by Adrian Saxe is one in a series of "antelope jars" that are among the "signature" vessels of the 1980s. These jars are at the esoteric end of the functional/nonfunctional pottery spectrum. They might hint

7
ADRIAN SAXE
LOS ANGELES, CA

Parisienne Chainsaw Massacre,
1982. Raku, stoneware and
porcelain. 25.25"H x 12"W x
7.25"D.

at some obscure function (containers for frankincense and myrrh perhaps) but in the end they are a hands-off experience. The antelope is deliberately fragile, with its curving horns and thin legs. Beside it, two exquisitely gilded chain-saw blades swoop out of the lid to act as handles; with their prickly sawtooth surface, the handles add to the object's "don't touch me, worship me" character.

What Saxe seeks to draw from the ceramic tradition is not easily encapsulated. The mystique of court porcelains, first manufactured in Europe in 1708, is at the heart of his vision. However, Saxe never set out to mimic these wares; rather, he was trying to project that heady essence of entitlement that they had once signified. Although Saxe does occasionally use handles and other elements actually cast from 250-year-old molds, most of his visual references come from banal everyday imagery: cog wheels, chain saws, douche wands and bar codes. Yet given the right lick of gold or platinum, these objects take on the majesty of court bibelots.

Saxe, too, tries to create hierarchy in his work. Each of the three "layers" (base, vessel and lid) represents a different plane of experience. The base of low-temperature raku-fired earthenware leaves the clay looking like soft, porous rock. The base of this piece has the shape of a small Mayan temple, but others in the series are organic in form and mimic the underground realms of earth, rock and lava. The vessel section represents the cultural realm of man. Appropriately, it is made of porcelain, which is not a natural clay dug from claybanks like earthenware and stoneware but rather a ceramic paste invented and compounded by man. Surmounting the third layer, a porcelain lid, is the high-fired stoneware antelope. It symbolizes nature, culture's adversary.

A note on patience. We waited nearly 20 years for *Parisienne Chainsaw Massacre* to enter our home. The piece was originally sold on Saxe's debut exhibition at our first gallery opposite the Los Angeles County Museum of Art in 1981. We were in love with the object from the day it arrived in the gallery and regretted selling it. But this pot never lost its magnetic pull and finally, a year ago, we had the opportunity to acquire the piece. Within minutes of being placed in our home it seemed as though it had always lived there, and conceptually at least, it always had.

Peter Voulkos's *Stack Pot* (fig. 4) is one of our collection's most major works in scale, importance and the stature of its maker. In 2002, after 78 riotous years of creativity, the ceramic world lost Voulkos to that great pottery in the sky. As the force behind the abstract expressionist ceramics movement, Voulkos did more than any other individual in the twentieth century to break through a media-based apartheid in the arts and establish a place for the vessel maker as a contemporary artist.

Like all of Voulkos's later work, the *Stack Pot* is fired in a Japanese-style wood-burning Anagama kiln. This is an arduous process during which the kiln has to be carefully fed wood for 24 to 48 hours. Interaction with the fire creates rich, scorched surfaces, replete with ash deposits, flame marks and vivid bursts of color. Wood firing is ceramics at its most pyrotechnic.

This method of firing, and the artistic credo of happenstance and serendipity that accompanies it, is Japanese in origin. Japanese pottery had the major impact on Voulkos, but one sees in his work specific influences of stoneware Bizen and Shigaraki wares, sixteenth- and seventeenth-century raku-fired tea bowls, pre-historic Jomon ware and, most emphatically, Haniwa figures with their cut-and-pierced volumes. However, Voulkos's pots are not to be confused with those made by Western Japanophiles who so felicitously try to mimic the classic wares of the islands' potters. Voulkos's homage to Japan is not through imitation but through transformation.

Like all of Voulkos's works, the *Stack Pot* is clearly Western, with its intrusive, muscular sensuality. The pot is magnificently thrown and its defining thick contours "move" fluidly around the form. This piece is precognitive; it's about feelings, not meanings. Watching Voulkos work was fascinating but so intense and intimate that at times one almost felt embarrassed, as though one had stumbled on a couple making love, which in a metaphoric sense was exactly the relationship between Voulkos and his wet, compliant clay.

And yet his manipulation of the surface—the cutting, piercing and reshaping—is vigorous, violent, almost an attack. In *Stack Pot*, a large crack is retained as part of the surface drawing and, indeed, it is one of the most impressive elements of the pot. Holes are everywhere. Holes themselves are not new to pottery, but Voulkos's approach to holes was new. He used them to release energy and to probe space. Some are penetrated from the outer mass into the interior volume (creating entrances) while others are from the inside out (exits). Objects have been impressed into the clay's surface, including an unlikely addition: a trail of tiny doll's feet. A small ball of clay originally attached to the pot was lost in shipping. We were upset, but Voulkos was unfazed about this changing "work-in progress," saying he was "never sure that clay lump was a good idea to begin with."

Each and every object in our collection carries a surprising weight of content, history, precedent and emotional bounty. It's a matter of how much one wants to access, how far one wants to explore. We could carry out this process of analysis with all of our favorites: Ralph Bacerra's unpretentious yet virtuosic decorative vessels; a Ron Nagle cup titled *New Julius* that glows like a red-hot ember just plucked from the fire; Anne Kraus's *Loving Cup* with its mix of decoration, poetry and dreamscape; a 1979 vessel by Richard DeVore, just five inches high, that holds its own against much larger pots in the collection. Karen Karnes's small single-stem flower vase is a marvel of design and sculptural presence. Then there are Geert Lap's sleek reductive pots, Babs Haenen's choreography of colored clay and Tony Marsh's vessel (the single most admired piece in our collection), in which he has drilled hundreds of holes and nearly removed the boundary between inner pot and outer pot, between volume and mass by making the perforated skin of his pots so literally porous.

The pots we use daily have the advantage of intimacy gained from regular touch. Garth begins every day with a hefty caffeine fix and uses either his David Shaner tea bowl with a thick, high-relief Mishima-style decoration or a large wood-fired porcelain cup by Gwyn Hanssen Pigott. Shaner's pot has achieved near perfection of form, as full around and generous as a half moon. Pigott's cup is both practical and texturally luxurious; the glaze feels like silk on the lips. Mark is less of a purist when choosing his morning coffee vessel and the guilty truth is that his favorite mug is commercial and carries a decal image of Doris Day. But this is an unrelated obsession; it belongs to another collection and requires its own essay.

Collecting and appreciating pots requires time. Some of the finest pots take a long time to give up their strength, and often there are surprises. One buys a pot for one reason, only to find out much later that its personality is very different from what one had initially imagined. This can be both good and bad. Generally pots are not like paintings and photographs, most of which project their message on their surfaces. The true secrets of pots are often hidden away in their enclosed interior space. They require the collector to reach in and extract their riches. Finding one's way through the aesthetic maze that makes up a great pot is not a simple matter.

Michael Cardew emphasized this point when he recounted an evening spent with Bernard Leach in St. Ives, when he was an apprentice. Leach held nightly post-dinner discussions with his students and staff about the virtues of specific pots. One evening Leach held up an inexpensive Korean rice bowl. It was not Imperial ware but the kind of vessel a laborer might own. "Look at it," Leach declared, "isn't it amazing how simple it is?" Tsuranosuke Matsubayashi, the scion and sixteenth generation of the Asahi family of potters, was present that evening, "on loan" to Leach from his friends in Japan to fix the terrible technical problems bedeviling his pottery. Leach's remark obviously bothered him and finally, summoning all the weight and wisdom of his long ceramic heritage, Matsubayashi countered, "No, I think it is very complicated."

And therein lies the test. If you cannot see a glimmer of the subtlety, charm, intelligence and even the grandeur that often resides in a bowl, a cup or a plate, then you are safe from "pot madness." However, the bad news is that you will also never gain access to the singular ecstasy of pot collecting. But if, in reading this essay or viewing the pots in this book, you feel a stirring, a sense of the depth of a pot's interior life—the richness of its visual intelligence, the embedded metaphors and symbolism, the tactile sensuality of its physical presence, the cultural associations in surface and shape, its swirling kinetic quality of line and the plastic manipulations of volume that verge on the erotic—not only are you at risk but you probably are already too far gone. If a passion for pots is indeed madness, then let us welcome you to the asylum.

ART UNCONTAINED

Preface

DOROTHY HAFNER
NEW YORK, NY

*Kyoto Homage platter, 1989.
White earthenware with applied
glazes. See page 62.*

Pots are containers. Some are meant to hold things, others to hold ideas. The two are not mutually exclusive, however, and both kinds of vessels are meant to be looked at and appreciated aesthetically. There are many different ways in which vessels can be approached visually, and this book is divided loosely according to those various approaches.

There are also two basic ways that pots can be conceived by the potter: the pot as a sculptural form, for which shape and glaze are the essential characteristics; and the pot as a canvas, on which the potter paints or draws. While there is a lot of overlap in these two groupings, they nonetheless remain distinct.

This book is not about art, nor is it a chronological history of studio ceramics.[1] It is, rather, a book about pottery and about what makes great pots. For the purposes of this essay, a pot is any vessel, any hollow container, whether functional or not. Of course, this essay is about how some pots can *be* art, and also about how, even in the humblest pots, there *is* art. It is a book about how the love of clay and its many properties makes it a compelling medium for a wide range of artistic exploration. Art cannot be contained within the rigid parameters of painting and sculpture; and the art of making great pots cannot be contained in any one aesthetic or tradition. For a curator as much as for the potter, that is part of the great appeal of pots.

Ulysses Grant Dietz
Curator, Decorative Arts, The Newark Museum

ART UNCONTAINED

The Studio Vessel from 1940 to 2002

This is a great pot.

We no longer know who Ruth Kenly is. We know nothing of her training as a potter, or what influenced her craft. We know only that she lived in Short Hills, New Jersey, and that this bowl (fig. 8) won first prize in the craft division of an arts festival held at The Newark Museum in 1959. We also know that the slip decoration was inspired by a pattern left on a window after her dog had licked it. We paid Mrs. Kenly $12 for the bowl in June 1959.

A first-rate pot need not be an "important" pot. This pot deserves careful study because of the remarkable finesse with which the rich, grainy stoneware body is brought up to a smooth, perfect, thin wall. The slight outward flare toward the base and the sharply undercut foot show a master's control of the medium. It is a wonderful, satisfying shape, not too heavy and not too light. It is a joy to hold in one's hand. Ruth Kenly knew how to throw. She also knew how to glaze, and how to decorate a piece in a way that was elegant, balanced and harmonious. The silky mauve and blue slips with which the decoration is applied complement beautifully the rusty brown of the ground. The bold yet delicate brushstrokes of the calligraphic decoration are graceful and deftly poised between rim and base. It seems effortless, and yet it is achieved with an expert precision rare for an amateur potter. It could be that Kenly's bowl—from its cylindrical form, like a large tea bowl, to the abstract calligraphic decoration— was inspired by the work of Shoji Hamada or Bernard Leach. But there is none of the slightly rough Japanese *mingei* or "folk" quality of Hamada's and Leach's work. One can see in the elegant form, so precisely potted, with its smooth surface and subtle glazes, something of the work of Gertrud and Otto Natzler or Edwin and Mary Scheier. It is a pot of which none of these potters would have been ashamed.

Clearly, Mrs. Kenly was not influenced by the radical departure from the traditional vessel that Peter Voulkos and his contemporaries were undertaking in California when she made this pot (see fig. 160). Mrs. Kenly was not cutting-edge, but she was, nonetheless, very much of her time. Her bowl exemplifies the best traditional studio pottery of the late 1950s.

While most museums and most collectors of contemporary ceramics might not look twice at Ruth Kenly's little pot from 1959, I hold it up to you as a work to be celebrated. It represents beauty, utility and wisdom. It does not startle or provoke, but it does give pleasure if one takes the time to look. It shows a love and understanding of clay and glaze, an intense personal interaction with the medium. It may not answer today's taste for the grand and the flamboyant, for the bold statement or the large gesture. Mrs. Kenly's bowl is modest, but even so it demands that we respect its greatness. It is everything a great pot should be, and the lesson it teaches can be applied to every piece discussed in this essay.

The qualities of beauty, utility and wisdom found in Mrs. Kenly's small pot are the three broadest themes of this book, and I want to proceed with an example of each.

ANNETTE CORCORAN
PACIFIC GROVE, CA

Montagu's Harrier, *2000. Painted porcelain. 12"H x 6"W x 5.25"D. See page 139.*

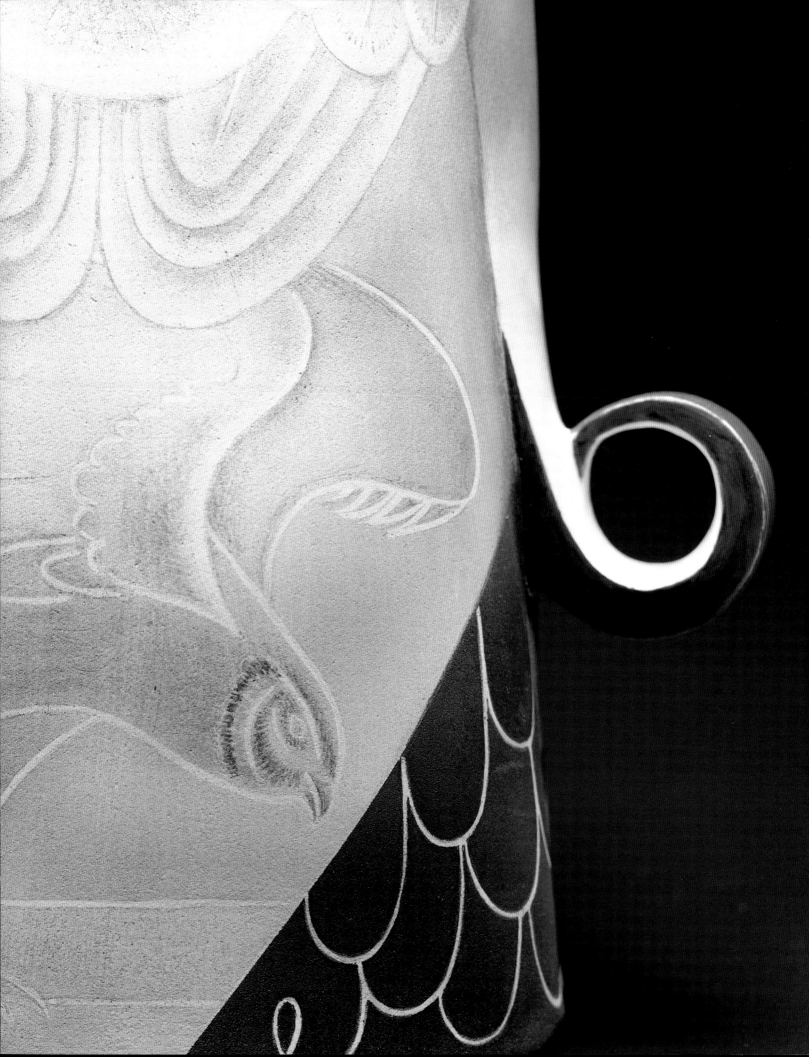

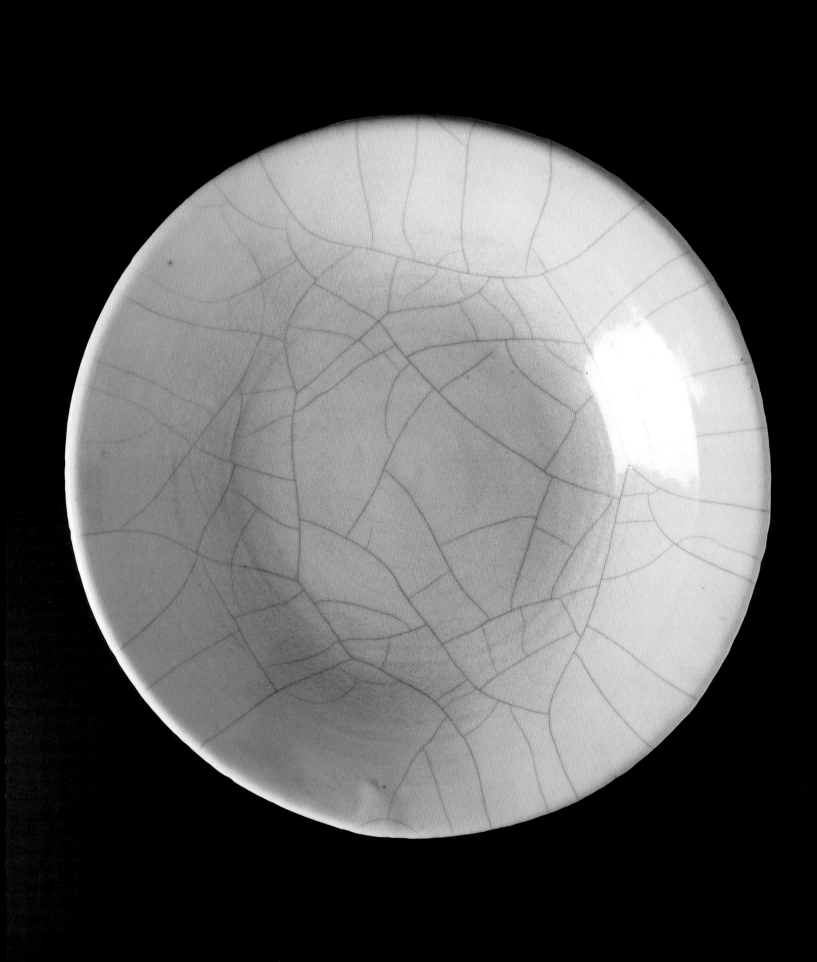

BEAUTY

Unlike "fine" art, a beautiful vessel can be an end and not just a means. Beauty is enough. Surface, form and technique are both necessary and sufficient for a beautiful pot. Utility is not necessarily excluded by beauty, nor is wisdom. But the self-sufficiency of beauty sometimes leaves no room (because there is no need) for anything else.

Glen Lukens was the most prominent figure of the early California studio pottery world, although his importance would later be overshadowed by the radical glamour and experimentation of the young potters of the 1950s in Los Angeles. For Lukens, beauty was the sole and sufficient goal, and he searched endlessly for ways to express the essential beauty of the vessel—with simple forms and extraordinary glazes. Lukens favored broad, shallow forms, simply potted and lavished with astonishingly rich coatings coaxed from his deep understanding of glaze chemistry.

Glen Lukens in his studio in Los Angeles. Courtesy of the Garth Clark Gallery.

9
GLEN LUKENS
LOS ANGELES, CA

Broad conical dish, 1930–40. Thrown earthenware with crackled custard yellow glaze. Purchase 1985 W. Clark Symington Bequest Fund (85.283). Purchased from the Garth Clark Gallery, New York City. 3"H x 15.25"Dia.

UTILITY

Edwin and Mary Scheier working in their studio in Durham, NH. Courtesy of the Mary and Ed Scheier Archive, Currier Gallery of Art, Manchester, NH.

10
EDWIN AND MARY SCHEIER
DURHAM, NH

Pitcher and one of three cups with rooster design, 1948. Thrown redware with blue glaze and sgraffito. Purchase 1949 Special Purchase Fund (49.372a–d). Purchased from the artists. Pitcher: 11.75"H x 6"Dia; cups: 4.5"H x 3.25"Dia.

The ancient root of all ceramic vessels is usefulness. In a museum such as this one, which collects objects that are part of everyday life, utilitarian studio vessels are an essential part of understanding the development of the art of pottery. It is through the utilitarian vessel that age-old traditions of pottery-making survive and evolve. Beauty is certainly not excluded by utility, and wisdom can also find its way into the making, but at bottom the useful vessel needs to at least *seem* to be well designed for its intended use.

Once upon a time, utility and art were not mutually exclusive. Edwin and Mary Scheier, one of the great American pottery couples of the past century, created pots that were works of art, and also pots that were meant to be used. The Scheiers did differentiate between their utilitarian "potboilers"[1] and their more self-consciously artistic pieces, but they applied the same standards of quality to everything that came out of their kiln. This beverage set (along with two other pieces, figs. 90 and 127) was purchased in 1949 from an exhibition at The Newark Museum called "The Decorative Arts Today." The museum's acquisition of pieces from this exhibition was focused on how an ordinary American family might use modern objects in their home.[2] This set was originally intended for serving lemonade. Its sleek modern forms are given a rustic, almost "early American" look with the use of simple sgraffito decoration. The essential modernity of form and decoration of these pieces was thus disguised in a comfortable old-fashioned housecoat. The craftsmanship, of course, is breathtaking, as good as any potting of its time. The Scheiers' technical approach to making pots was influenced equally by the seminal writings by Charles Fergus Binns, founder of the Alfred University School of Clayworking, and by Bernard Leach's landmark publication, *A Potter's Book*.[3]

WISDOM

Wisdom is an especially rich characteristic of studio vessels of the past half century or so. Wisdom denotes intelligence and thought, but a wise pot can also provoke a smile of understanding, an "aha" moment. Wisdom often involves wit or humor; it can be rebellious, or it can invoke a deeply spiritual, worshipful emotion. Wisdom often—intentionally—precludes, or at least interferes with, utility. Beauty, too, becomes a relative thing with a wise pot, although beauty can be a subversive tool in a wise potter's hands.

Adrian Saxe in his studio in Los Angeles. Courtesy of the Garth Clark Gallery.

With its opulent glazes, sly reference to Chinese-character wine pots of the eighteenth century,[4] and cactus finial evoking the deserts of Southern California, Adrian Saxe's teapot exemplifies the wisdom of so much postmodern ceramics in America. This piece pays serious homage to historical porcelains of the Old World and Asia, and at the same time presents a whimsical, even kitschy approach to design that draws deeply on the pop culture of Saxe's childhood and youth. It pokes fun at the seriousness of ceramic history while embracing the academic knowledge that, for a curator, ties all ceramics together.

11
ADRIAN SAXE
LOS ANGELES, CA

Ampersand Teapot, *1988. Porcelain with celadon glaze and platinum luster. Gift of Garth Clark and Mark Del Vecchio, 1989 (89.88a, b). 10.5"H x 9"W x 2.75"D.*

THE BEAUTIFUL POT

THE BEAUTIFUL POT

Beauty is hardly a monolithic standard. All of the pots in this section are beautiful, even though they vary widely in style. We can begin with two remarkable early matriarchs in American studio ceramics, Maija Grotell and Rose Gonzales (figs. 12 and 13). These women approached beauty in very different ways in the late 1930s. Grotell brought Finnish modernism to America and transformed the way ceramic art students looked at the vessel. She taught her students to love the "search" that was part of making a pot. Two of her students, Richard DeVore and Toshiko Takaezu, have exemplified that lesson in their long careers. The strong graphic design and high-contrast black and white of Grotell's vase place it firmly in the so-called moderne aesthetic of the late 1930s. Yet the technical qualities of throwing and glaze follow the well-established tradition of both European and American studio pottery of the 1920s, with its adherence to the idea of the "perfect pot" based on Asian models.[5]

Gonzales's concept of beauty, on the other hand, came out of the rebirth of ancient Native American ceramic traditions in the 1920s and '30s. Unlike Grotell, Gonzales was not part of an academic world, and she viewed her pots as a means of subsistence for herself and her family. Like Grotell, however, Gonzales searched for her own inspiration within her native tradition. She claimed to have invented the carved technique that has become an earmark of both San Ildefonso and Santa Clara Pueblo pottery.[6] Her stylized, geometrical decoration, simple shapes and sleek, polished surfaces were entirely sympathetic with the high-style art deco designs that were establishing currency in Euro-American culture during the 1920s and '30s. The Newark Museum collected Indian pottery in the 1920s much in the same way it collected folk art—partly because of its historical/ethnographic interest and partly because of its strikingly modernist aesthetic.

12
MAIJA GROTELL
NEW BRUNSWICK, NJ

Cylindrical vase in modernist style, 1937. Thrown stoneware with applied dark brown and white glazes. Purchase 1997 Felix Fuld Bequest Fund and Membership Endowment Fund (97.77). Purchased from Historical Design, Inc., New York City. 10.25"H x 7.5"Dia.

13
ROSE GONZALES
SAN ILDEFONSO PUEBLO, NM

Bowl with plumed serpent,
ca. 1940. Coiled and carved
earthenware. Purchase 1979
Sophronia Anderson Bequest Fund
(79.622). Purchased from the
Mudd-Carr Gallery, Santa Fe,
NM. 3.9"H x 4.6"Dia.

Both of these women became teachers for succeeding generations of pot-ters—in Gonzales's case, her own descendants—and both of them created works that exemplified a modern concept of beauty for the time in which they worked.

THE CLASSIC POT

The classic pot is the kind of pot that is archetypal; it evokes past traditions and techniques. There is often a timeless quality about the classic pot, making it hard to date precisely. Observe, for example, the relationship between the vases in figures 14 and 15, by a famous teacher and her famous student. Grotell's hare's-fur vase was probably produced just around the time she began teaching at the

14
MAIJA GROTELL
BLOOMFIELD HILLS, MI

Ovoid vase, ca. 1940. Thrown stoneware with hare's-fur glaze. Gift of Garth Clark and Mark Del Vecchio, 1985 (85.282). 8.25"H x 7.5"Dia.

15
TOSHIKO TAKAEZU
CLINTON, NJ

Vase, 1964. Thrown stoneware with painted decoration. Purchase 1965 (65.216). Purchased from the artist. 10.25"H x 8.75"Dia.

Cranbrook Academy in Bloomfield Hills, Michigan, and it represents a vivid homage to Asian forms and glaze techniques. This piece, subtle yet elegant and even opulent in its simplicity, parallels the work of Grotell's contemporaries Bernard Leach and Shoji Hamada, although at this early date their work was not yet widely known in this country. American studio potters of the 1920s and '30s were still influenced heavily by Japanese and Korean prototypes, and this work seems to be a part of that ongoing tradition.

Takaezu is considered the heir to Grotell's legacy as a teacher. This early vase (fig. 15) was purchased by The Newark Museum in 1965. Made a generation later than her teacher's example, it stands poised at the crossroads of Toshiko's career, echoing the still-functional forms of her mentor while giving clear indication that Takaezu saw the vessel as something other than a thing simply to be used. The subtle asymmetrical shaping of the body and the abstract painting on the surface—both of which evoke seventeenth-century Japanese *Oribe* tea wares—indicate the sculptural and painterly qualities that would dominate Takaezu's work from this point onward. It is tempting to see the influence of American abstract expressionist painting in the surface treatment of Takaezu's vase; however, the debt it owes to the abstract glazing of Japanese pottery is undeniable.

Bernard Leach was the master of contemporary classic pots. His interest in all traditional pottery grew from the fact that he was a child of the British arts and crafts movement of the late nineteenth century and despised the effect of industrialization on ceramic design.[7] All through his career his work harked back to the 1920s, when he began his association with Japanese master potter Shoji Hamada. This vase (fig. 16), although a knowledgeable evocation of an ancient Chinese form and decorative technique, is iconic of Leach's style, and it embodies the characteristics that made him a leading influence. The beautifully controlled volume of the body swells outward and then tapers gracefully in to an elegant but solid base. The carefully wrought reel at the rim, modeled on Chinese prototypes, echoes the dark brown lines of varying thickness that encircle the body. The simply yet eloquently painted leaping salmon freezes an instant of time. One almost waits to hear the "plop" as the fish falls back into the water. The whole piece creates a vivid image of the potter at work: the spinning potter's wheel, the slip-loaded brush, the bucket of creamy white glaze.

The generous scale of Waistel Cooper's baluster-form vase of about the same period (fig. 17) gives the classical Chinese form of this vase a modern presence.

17
WAISTEL COOPER
PORLOCK, ENGLAND

*Baluster-form vase, 1960. Thrown
earthenware with gray glaze.
Purchase 1960 (60.497). Purchased
from Heal & Son, Ltd., London.
12.5"H x 9.75"Dia.*

18
MARVIN BLACKMORE
DOLORES, CO

*Water jar, 2000. Thrown and
carved earthenware. Purchase
2001 Members' Fund and Estate of
Alice G. and Fred W. Radel
(2001.71). Purchased from the
artist. 11"H x 9"Dia.*

Meant to hold a large-scale spray of flowers or foliage, it would have been appropriate in its color and its size for the open interiors common in modern homes of the postwar period. Its oriental form, with the uneven glaze characteristic of ancient pots, was comforting to cold war consumers.

The same shape appears 40 years later in the work of Marvin Blackmore, a young Native American potter working in Colorado. He merges the classic oriental form (fig. 18) with his own spin on American Indian motifs—intricate repeated designs drawn from native iconography and carved through multiple layers of colored slip. The embellished surfaces of this piece suggest an almost Victorian love of decoration, recalling late-nineteenth-century American interiors. The marvelous, obsessive quality of the labor also brings to mind Adelaide Alsop Robineau's needle-carved porcelains from the early twentieth century.[8] Thus Blackmore celebrates his own heritage, but he does so in a way that departs radically from the native traditions that inspire him.

Harrison McIntosh's classic bottles and vases of the 1960s (fig. 19) are inspired by natural elements, especially wind and water.[9] The sinuous stripes on this bottle are totally in sync with graphic design and textiles of the mid-1960s. And yet this piece also appears to be inspired by eighteenth-century Japanese wares. A student of Glen Lukens in the early 1940s, McIntosh draws inspiration from many directions, including seemingly disparate models such as Bernard Leach, the Bauhaus and Peter Voulkos. However classic his work appears to be, it is the product of a pot-making ethos like no other in America.

Brother Thomas, on the other hand, pays conscious homage to archetypal Chinese forms and glazes (fig. 20), linking their spiritual foundation to his own experience as a Benedictine monk.[10] To him, his classically shaped and glazed pots are living, breathing things. He is a master of every arcane Chinese glaze formula and has endlessly explored variations on classic vase shapes over the past several decades. New Jerseyan Al Green spent his entire career in pursuit of the painterly qualities found in Japanese stoneware, resisting all distractions. Green found enough abstract expressionism in his painterly glazes to satisfy his desire for modernity (see the large plate in fig. 34). Elva Nampeyo's classic pot, with its fluid opposed-bird-wing motifs (fig. 22), echoes the dynastic style begun by her Hopi grandmother, Nampeyo. As with traditional Japanese and Chinese potters, the act of emulation honors Hopi heritage and keeps a cultural legacy alive.[11]

19
HARRISON MCINTOSH
CLAREMONT, CA

Striped bottle vase, 1967–68. Thrown stoneware with wax-resist glaze. Purchase 1993 Emma Fantone Endowment Fund for Decorative Arts (93.91). Purchased from Studio Potter *magazine. 12"H x 5"Dia.*

20 *(opposite)*
**BROTHER THOMAS
(THOMAS BEZANSON)**
WESTON PRIORY, VT

Canteen vase, 1991. Handbuilt porcelain with saffron-iron glaze. Purchase 1992 Decorative Arts Purchase Fund (92.318). Purchased from the Pucker Gallery, Boston, MA. 10.5"H x 8.75"W x 3.5"D.

21
ALBERT GREEN
WESTFIELD, NJ

Square bottle vase, 1989. Handbuilt stoneware. Purchase 1990 Margaret D. Batt Bequest Fund (90.217). Purchased from the artist from an exhibition at The Newark Museum. 10.7"H x 7.5"W x 2.75"D.

22
ELVA NAMPEYO
HOPI PUEBLO, AZ

Jar with painted decoration, 1960s. Coiled earthenware. Gift of Dr. Edwin R. Littmann, 1967 (67.422). 4.5"H x 6.5"Dia.

47

The painterly pot does not necessarily negate the importance of form, but the decoration becomes paramount in the pot's meaning and its beauty. Two early examples of rather different scale demonstrate this. Beatrice Wood's masterpiece from the 1940s (fig. 23) is hardly more than a circular canvas for her neo-cubistic painting of musicians. The emphasis is on the design and the colors she obtained with tin alkali glazes.[12] The subject is taken from the modern art she knew well from her years among the avant-garde in Europe. This plate came to The Newark Museum very early—perhaps the first piece of her pottery in an American museum—and it is interesting to note that it came to us not from a pottery collector but from a modern-art collector.

Henry Varnum Poor was himself a painter, but he turned to pottery because of its inherent physical qualities and the possibilities for self-expression it offered (fig. 24). He relished the rugged and primitive nature of the handmade pot. Some of Poor's more ambitious plates and bowls were intended as contemplative "art" objects, but in the manner of Shoji Hamada's *mingei* (folk) pottery, much of his work was made and sold to be useful.[13] Part of the appeal of ceramics for artists like Poor was the fact that the work could be used, thus elevating humble, everyday activities. Poor valued highly the uniqueness of each handmade pot, the inherent beauty of even the most humble vessel.

Shoji Hamada, like his friend and colleague Bernard Leach, studied European as well as Asian folk art and from that study found the inspiration for his pots. As Leach consciously nurtured the English tradition of craftsmen potters in St. Ives, Hamada did the same in his Mashiko, Japan, compound. Sometimes his masterful, abstract painting decorated "showpieces" (fig. 25), but he lavished equal care on modest pieces meant for domestic use (fig. 26). This kind of painterly, nonrepresentational decoration seems very modern but is in fact very ancient. It appealed to modernists in the 1940s and '50s, and must have helped Hamada's influence take root in America.

The other side of this painterly influence is easy to see in the painted plate from 1957 by Fong Chow, a teacher at the New York State College of Ceramics at Alfred University (fig. 27). Almost but not quite abstract, the stripped-down,

23
BEATRICE WOOD
OJAI, CA

Large plate with cubist design of musicians, 1940–47. Earthenware with tin alkaline glazes. Gift of Mr. and Mrs. C. Suydam Cutting, 1948 (48.328). 2.25"H x 16"Dia.

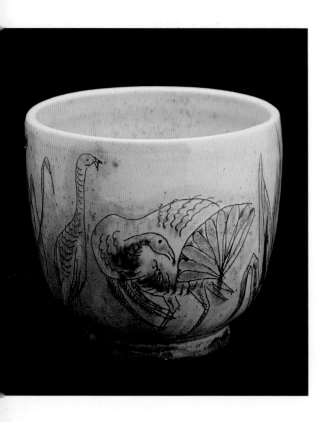

24
HENRY VARNUM POOR
NEW CITY, NY

Bowl with design of wild turkeys,
1948. Thrown earthenware with
sgraffito decoration. Gift of the
Forbes Foundation 1985 (85.6).
Purchased from the Garth Clark
Gallery, New York City. 5.4"H x
6"Dia.

25
SHOJI HAMADA
MASHIKO, JAPAN

Plate with painted decoration,
1940–50. Stoneware with temmoku
glaze. Purchase 1979 Felix Fuld
Bequest Fund (79.169). Purchased
at Toyobi Gallery, New York City.
2.5"H x 13.25"Dia.

26
SHOJI HAMADA
MASHIKO, JAPAN

Deep bowl, 1946–51. Thrown
stoneware with painted decoration.
Purchase 1952 (52.66). Purchased
from Kogei Gallery, New York
City. 4.75"H x 7.9"Dia.

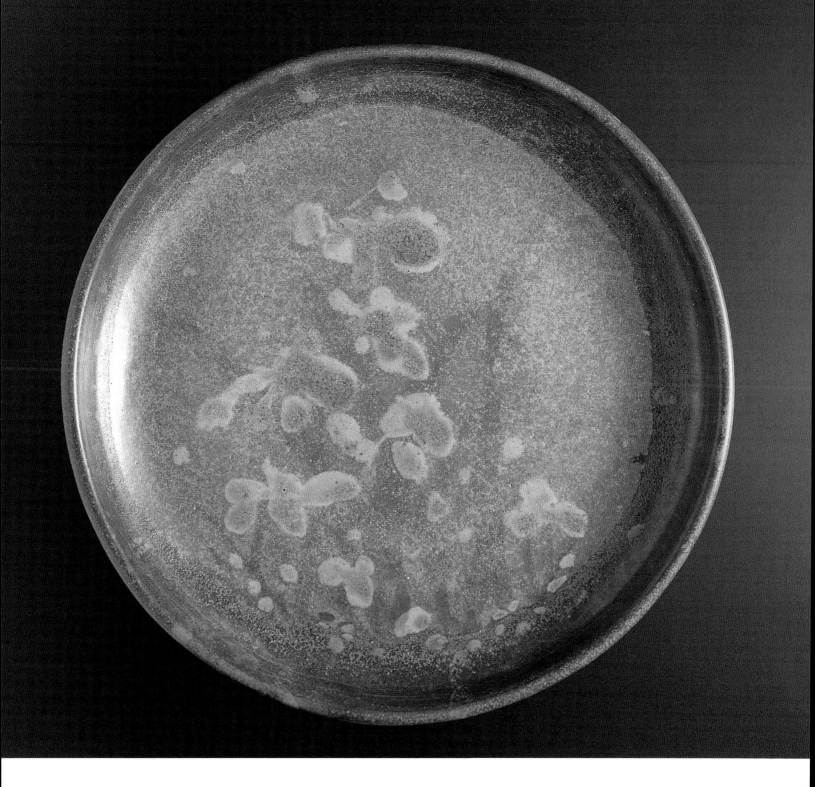

27
FONG CHOW
ALFRED, NY

Plate with iris motif, 1957.
Stoneware with slip painting.
Purchase 1957 (57.150). Purchased
from an exhibition at the Museum
of Contemporary Crafts, New York
City. 1.25"H x 13"Dia.

28
JOHN GLICK
FARMINGTON HILLS, MI

*Large bowl, 1992. Thrown
stoneware with painted decoration.
Purchase 1992 Mathilde Oestrich
Bequest Fund (92.242). Purchased
from the Garth Clark Gallery, New
York City. 7.25"H x 23"Dia.*

exquisitely controlled painting evokes seventeenth-century Japanese *Mino* ware
with its calligraphic image of an iris.[14] This sort of representation was also very
current in the 1950s but has in recent years been increasingly seen as un-modern
and somehow less "important" due to the overweening influence of abstract
expressionism. Chow's work parallels that of John Glick, another student of
Maija Grotell, whose lush painterly bowl (fig. 28) not only evokes eighteenth-
century ceramic forms, but offers highly stylized and colorful images of flowers
in what at first seems to be an entirely abstract design.

The painterly pot can of course also be a sculptural pot, especially when the
form is critical to the effect of the painting. If Beatrice Wood's large platter
diminishes the importance of the form to a mere backdrop, other potters did
the opposite. Katherine Choy, who died an untimely death in 1958 at the age of
29, was a master glaze chemist. In this minimalist vase from 1957–58 (fig. 29),
Choy used her two best-known glazes in combination: celadon and copper red.
The square brushstrokes recall the calligraphic work of traditional Asian potters,

but their blunt rectangular form is altogether more modern. The austere shape of the vase is essential to the effectiveness of this painting; it wouldn't work as well on a flat form such as a plate.

Conversely, Swedish master potter Wilhelm Kåge makes the most of a thick, double-walled plate form to create dazzling glaze effects (fig. 30). One could argue that this is a purely sculptural piece, since there is no drawing of any sort, but the potter clearly had painterly intentions when he applied the turquoise and green glazes to this redware form. The technically difficult double-walled construction of this plate removes it from the company of ordinary flat dishes. Its increased mass and thickness give it a three-dimensional heft and presence.

29
KATHERINE CHOY
PORT CHESTER, NY

Vase, 1957–58. Thrown porcelain with celadon and copper-red glazes. Promised gift of the Choy family, 2002 (TR122.2000.2). 10.5"H x 5"Dia.

A very different piece by Katherine Choy, also from 1957–58 (fig. 31), complements a biomorphic form with a collage-like application of engobes. The result is very "fifties," whereas Choy's celadon vase with red brushmarks (previous page) would be impossible to date purely by style. Toshiko Takaezu's garden seat form of 1971 (fig. 32) clearly melds form and painted decoration. The brushstrokes are shaped by the curves of the vessel, as are Janet Leach's large painterly sweeps of glaze on her magnificent vessel from 1965 (fig. 33). Al Green, who used a fairly limited number of shapes during his many years as a potter, often used a large, flat charger as a canvas for his painting. This piece (fig. 34) recalls the abstract expressionist gestures of contemporary artists such as Norman Bluhm and Robert Motherwell.

An entirely different sort of painterly quality began to appear in American studio pots in the late 1970s. Ralph Bacerra was one of the first potters to revive the highly decorative surface, turning to enamels and luster glazes in a way that would have been unheard of in Los Angeles (or anywhere else in the

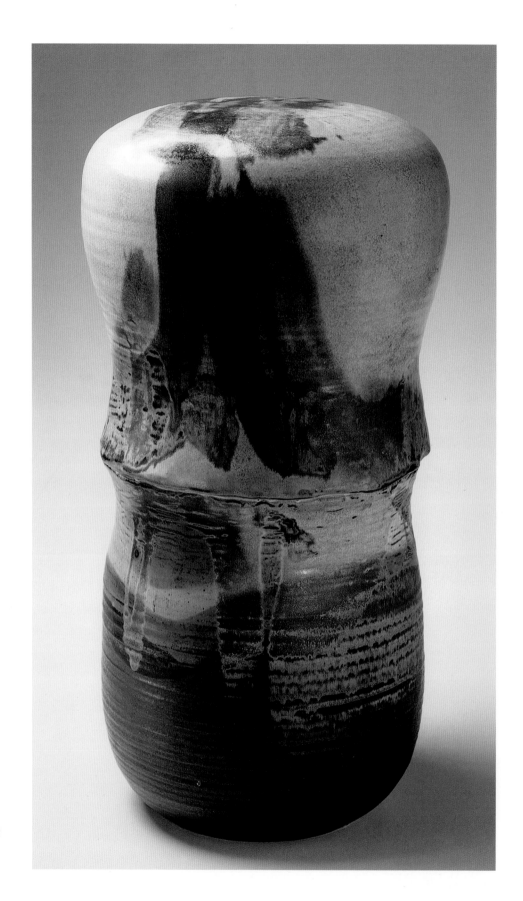

32
TOSHIKO TAKAEZU
CLINTON, NJ

Large closed form (garden seat),
1971. Thrown stoneware with
painted decoration. Purchase 1971
Thomas L. Raymond Bequest Fund
(71.70). Purchased from the artist.
19.25"H x 9.75"Dia.

33
JANET LEACH
ST. IVES, ENGLAND

Large vase with gray and tan glazes, 1965–66. Thrown stoneware with painted decoration. Purchase 1966 (66.426). Purchased from Primavera Gallery, London. 15"H x 15.5"Dia.

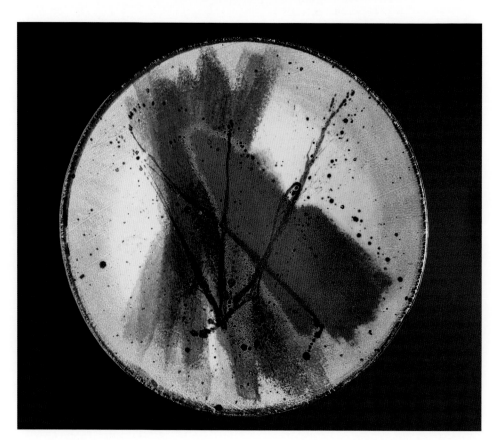

34
ALBERT GREEN
WESTFIELD, NJ

Large plate, 1975. Stoneware with painted decoration. Purchase 1975 Felix Fuld Bequest Fund (75.118). Purchased from the artist. 3"H x 20.5"Dia.

Western world, for that matter) a decade earlier. A porcelain plate from 1976 (fig. 3) echoes the scalloped dish forms of eighteenth-century Asian export wares, while his swirling, richly colored enamels seem to meld refined Japanese *kutani* wares with the psychedelic imagery of the 1960s. From the viewpoint of a decorative arts curator, the piece suggests a revival of the Japanism of the 1870s, demonstrating, as it does, the same intense fascination with complex decoration and color schemes.

The painted decoration for which Toshiko Furukawa is famous, seen here on an elegant box from 1987 (fig. 35), brings to mind the glamorous woven and embroidered textiles of eighteenth-century Japanese kimonos. Working in the same Japanese town where Shoji Hamada's studio was located, Furukawa purposefully contrasts her delicate, asymmetrical painting with the severe geometry of her characteristic box forms.[15] Furukawa's brushwork, however, is not a revival of anything, but a survival of a tradition of painterly decoration in Japan.

When Dorothy Hafner began to produce her *Kyoto Homage* line of studio tablewares in the 1980s (fig. 36), she looked to the same kind of sources that

35
TOSHIKO FURUKAWA
MASHIKO, JAPAN

Covered square box, 1987. Handbuilt stoneware with painted decoration. Gift of Joan B. Mirviss, 1987 (87.207a, b). 1.5"H x 6.8"W x 6.8"D.

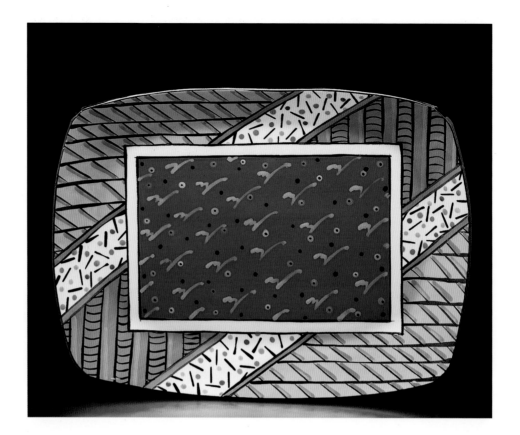

inspired Furukawa. The result, however, is more electric, more self-consciously urban and modern, recalling the static patterns on a television screen as much as they do the Japanese motifs honored in her title. A later and larger plate by Ralph Bacerra (fig. 37) continues to evoke the elaborate enameled porcelains of the eighteenth and nineteenth centuries, but here the iconography seems to have turned toward a Peter Max–meets–M.C. Escher swirl of birds and checkerboards. On this plate, as on the large plates by Beatrice Wood and Albert Green (figs. 23 and 34), the clay has become a canvas, and the form is secondary to the decoration.

Rondina Huma, however, like Toshiko Furukawa, works in a traditional context. The iconography of Huma's coiled and painted jar (fig. 38) is taken from Hopi imagery, but Huma has fragmented her images and rearranged them in a complex pattern suggestive of potsherds—fragments of her own cultural traditions reinterpreted for a modern world.[16]

Both Blue Corn and Lolita Concho work with abstract designs in their painterly pots. While these designs are drawn from traditional Native American images, it is not their iconography that matters to the potter. Blue Corn (fig. 39)

38
RONDINA HUMA
HOPI PUEBLO, AZ

*Jar with painted decoration, 1979.
Coiled earthenware with applied
engobes. Purchase 1979 Franklin
Conklin, Jr., Bequest Fund
(79.626). Purchased from the
Mudd-Carr Gallery, Santa Fe,
NM. 4.15"H x 5.5"Dia.*

39
BLUE CORN
SAN ILDEFONSO PUEBLO, NM

*Jar with polychrome decoration,
1983. Coiled earthenware with
applied engobes. Purchase 1983 The
Members' Fund (83.49). Purchased
from the artist. 6.5"H x 6.75"Dia.*

40 *(opposite)*
LOLITA CONCHO
ACOMA PUEBLO, NM

*Canteen with painted decoration,
ca. 1980. Coiled earthenware with
applied engobes. Purchase 1983
The Members' Fund (83.423).
Purchased from Letta Wofford
Gallery, Santa Fe, NM. 9"H x 9"W
x 8"D.*

41
BENNETT BEAN
BLAIRSTOWN, NJ

*Large painted vessel, 1989.
Handbuilt earthenware with
applied glazes, paint and gold leaf.
Purchase 1989 The Members' Fund
(89.86). Purchased from the artist,
from an exhibition at The Newark
Museum. 9.5"H x 16.25"W x
16.15"D.*

is credited with reintroducing polychrome pots to San Ildefonso, where the shiny, all-black vessel popularized by Maria Martinez in the 1920s had all but driven out the polychrome tradition. Blue Corn drew inspiration from historic pieces of polychrome ware that she saw in museums.[17] Concho, working in the black-and-white tradition of the Acoma Pueblo, was inspired by prehistoric pieces (fig. 40). The success of each of these great pots depends not upon being able to understand the symbols, but entirely on the graphic skill of the potter-painter and her ability to conform the designs to the shape of the vessel. As Native American artists, they draw from the deep well of their own cultural heritage, but their ultimate goal is to please the eye with perfectly wrought shapes and brilliantly executed designs.

Similarly, on Bennett Bean's large vessel of 1989 (fig. 41), the cloud-like glaze designs achieved through the wood-firing process have no "meaning," per se. The gilded crosses and painted geometric forms are pure abstractions, placed on the outer surface of the pot for visual effect. Like its two Indian counterparts, it is a three-dimensional abstract painting. None of these pieces is meant to be useful, even though all three use the form of traditional utilitarian pots. Bean has gone so far as to gold-leaf the interior, creating a surface that rejects function and also turns the eye to the exterior. These are vessels meant to hold their makers' aspirations.

66

Landscape is not a theme generally incorporated into contemporary ceramics, but the two nonfunctional vessels shown here evoke landscape in both two and three dimensions. Sculptural and painterly at once, the work of Wayne Higby calls up mountain vistas and deep gorges (fig. 42). Using a very different technique, Zenji Miyashita layers subtly colored clay (fig. 43) in distinctly non-traditional forms to give the sense of misty mountains seen from the air. Although Miyashita's *Small Boot* could ostensibly hold flowers, Higby's landscape, by virtue of flowing from interior to exterior, denies function.

The very idea of a painterly pot evokes color: glazes, slips, enamels. But the skilled use of black-and-white decoration can transform a piece into a striking three-dimensional drawing rather than a sculptural painting. The black-and-white format is a distinctive tradition with the potters of the Acoma Pueblo in New Mexico. Marie Chino, part of a celebrated potting family, contrasts thin hatched lines with black geometric shapes against a brilliant white slip (fig. 44).

42
WAYNE HIGBY
ALFRED, NY

Gray Sand Basin, *1977. Raku-fired earthenware. Gift of Linda Leonard Schlenger, 1996 (96.93). 12.75"H x 22"W x 12.6"D.*

43
ZENJI MIYASHITA
KYOTO, JAPAN

Small Boot *vase, 1985. Handbuilt
stoneware. Gift of Dr. and Mrs.
Frederick Baekeland, 1989
(89.671). 14.75"H x 4.6"W x
3.75"D.*

It's easy to see how such a bold graphic statement would have been popular in the 1960s and '70s, when strong, two-dimensional pop art graphics were part of mainstream aesthetics. At the beginning of the twenty-first century, however, it might just be the pot's classic timelessness that holds its deepest appeal to the non-Indian viewer. It evokes past generations of pot painters, in much the same way that traditionalist Japanese studio pottery does, and draws on that association for its emotional allure.

In a modernist updating of the Acoma fine-line tradition, Marie Chino works with her daughter, Vera Chino Ely, who paints Marie's coiled vessel with an eye-dazzling pattern entirely in thinly spaced freehand black lines (fig. 45). The shape is based on that of a traditional Acoma seed storage jar, but the design is a new interpretation of a traditional idea. It brings to mind the colorful paintings produced by op artists such as Richard Anuszkiewicz during the 1960s.

Although there is certainly precedence for a monochromatic presentation in Euro-American studio pottery (see the two Scheier pieces from 1948, figs. 90 and 127), the extraordinary pots of David Regan and Edward Eberle have a very new—even postmodern—quality. Perhaps the development of the black ceramic ink with which these two potters draw on their vessels made this quality possible; nevertheless, each artist has created a startlingly different spin on the painterly pot. In both Regan's and Eberle's work, the vessel is as important as the drawing, just as it is for the Acoma potters. Regan's surreal fish tureen from 1995 (fig. 46) is a complex porcelain vessel, thrown and built and modeled, then *detailed* with fine black line drawing. There is a parallel in the silversmithing world of repoussé chasing. The silversmith roughs out a silver shape by hammering out from the inside; then he fills in all the fine details on the outside with a chasing tool. Regan has done the same thing with porcelain and ink. The historical precedent behind this form is found in eighteenth-century Portuguese faience, in which a fish tureen is made in the form of a wooden bucket of freshly caught fish, and then painted in naturalistic tin-glaze colors.[18] Regan's piece exudes the same sort of whimsy as its prototype, right down to the platinum luster puddle that forms the tray. The black-and-white scheme, however, makes the piece feel like an old snapshot, as if this net bag full of dripping fish is a memory from the artist's own past, or from some shared historical past. This sculpture pays homage to the delightful European tradition of porcelain

44
MARIE Z. CHINO
ACOMA PUEBLO, NM

Olla with painted decoration,
1980. Coiled earthenware with
applied engobes. Purchase 1979
Sophronia Anderson Bequest Fund
(79.623). Purchased from the
Mudd-Carr Gallery, Santa Fe,
NM. 8"H x 10"Dia.

45
MARIE Z. CHINO AND
VERA CHINO ELY
ACOMA PUEBLO, NM

Seed jar with fine-line decoration,
1980. Coiled earthenware with
applied engobes. Purchase 1979
Sophronia Anderson Bequest Fund
(79.624). Purchased from the
Mudd-Carr Gallery, Santa Fe,
NM. 6"H x 7.5"Dia.

46
DAVID REGAN
MISSOULA, MT

Fish Tureen, 1995. Thrown and handbuilt porcelain with black stain. Purchase 1995 The Members' Fund (95.102a–c). Purchased from the Garth Clark Gallery, New York City. Tureen: 15"H x 15.5"Dia; tray: 0.4"H x 16.25"W x 16"D.

47
EDWARD EBERLE
PITTSBURGH, PA

The Weaver and the Woven, *1999. Thrown and altered porcelain with black stain. Purchase 2002 Membership Endowment Fund and John J. O'Neill Bequest Fund (2002.23.9a, b). Purchased from the Garth Clark Gallery, New York City. 17.5"H x 11.75"W x 10.5"D.*

tureens that advertised the ingredients served inside. Using Regan's tureen, however, would be a challenge.

Eberle, born in 1944, at the opposite end of the baby boom from Regan, creates an altogether more mythical and mystical world with his architectural vessel (fig. 47). Seeming to evoke Okinawan house form burial urns, or even ancient Etruscan funerary caskets, Eberle's title, *The Weaver and the Woven*, doesn't explain the piece so much as suggest the possibilities of meaning. It's as if this vessel—thrown and then altered to its square shape—is a representation of an ancient house, and the drawings are wall paintings. It is a reliquary for a complex, and perhaps unhappy, story. The drawings are as darkly rich as engravings by Rembrandt or Dürer, yet nightmarish in their complicated, inexplicable detail.[19]

THE SCULPTURAL POT

As we've already seen, painterly pots are sculptural too. This section, however, is devoted to pots that rely on clay and glaze to make their visual and emotional impact. What better place to begin than in 1944 with a spectacular bowl by Otto and Gertrud Natzler (fig. 48). Unlike many of their peers, the Natzlers considered all of their work, large and small (see fig. 72), to be objects of contemplation; they did not see it as functional ware. The dramatically thin potting and subtle shaping of this bowl (with its rich "patina" glaze evoking a weathered bronze) exemplify the streamlined, biomorphic shapes of the postwar years. You could stretch a point and say that the sweeping lines of the rim recall the work of artists such as Jose de Rivera, but that would be begging the question. Sculptural or not, this piece is all about being a bowl—an exquisite, function-defying, perfectly thrown and glazed bowl. It is to 1940s pots what a perfect white carved bowl was to Sung potters in tenth-century China: a precious object to be revered and treasured.

48 *(opposite)*
OTTO AND **GERTRUD**
NATZLER
LOS ANGELES, CA

Large folded bowl, 1944. Thrown
stoneware with patina glaze.
Purchase 1949 (49.374). Purchased
from the Van Dieman-Lilienfeld
Galleries, New York City. 4.6"H x
13.75"W x 10.6"D.

49
ROLF KEY-ØBERG
DENMARK

Ovoid folded bowl, 1948.
Handbuilt stoneware with textured
black glaze. Purchase 1949
(49.369). Purchased from the
Bertha Schaeffer Galleries, New
York City. 3"H x 13.25"W x 11.9"D.

Next to the Natzlers' piece, Danish potter Rolf Key-Øberg's folded bowl of 1948 (fig. 49) seems heavier, earthier, more likely to be *used*. But like the Natzlers, he relies on the subtle curves of the uplifted sides of his dish and textured charcoal-gray glaze to make his pot beautiful in a very 1940s moderne way. The swirling abstract line that meanders across the dish might seem painterly, but clearly it is secondary to form and glaze. Both of these pieces came out of the 1948 exhibition at The Newark Museum, "The Decorative Arts Today," and reflect the way that seemingly traditional vessels could defy utility without seeming radical.

Lucie Rie's gorgeous lipped bowl, made in 1959 (fig. 50) and purchased in London by The Newark Museum in 1960, carries on this tradition. Rie's pots are usually associated with perfect symmetry, and this asymmetrical bowl seems to cry out for pancake batter to be poured from it onto a hot griddle. One wants this piece to have been made *for a purpose*, and to go with her other functional wares (see the coffeepot in fig. 114). Ultimately, however, it is meant to be "used" only visually, to bring aesthetic pleasure to whoever appreciates its grace and elegance.

50
LUCIE RIE
LONDON, ENGLAND

Bowl, 1959. Thrown stoneware with speckled white glaze. Purchase 1960 (60.496). Purchased from Heal & Son, Ltd., London. 5.75"H x 10.5"W x 8.7"D.

51
HANS COPER
LONDON, ENGLAND

White vessel with wide flanged rim,
1970–74. Thrown stoneware.
Collection of Vivian and Martin
Levin. 8.25"H x 6.5"W x 6"D.

The legendary Hans Coper worked with elegant, austere forms that were technically functional but invariably totemic, seemingly imbued with some archaic power regardless of their size (see fig. 75). It is hard to imagine anyone popping a handful of daisies into this small but powerful vessel from the early 1970s (fig. 51). The monochromatic surfaces—either white or black—shimmer with subtle texture and gradations of color, looking as if they've been carved from stone. But Coper always made pots, and—uniquely among his peers—his pots were always seen as sculpture.

The same qualities seen in Coper's work are very much part of the carved, coiled black pots of the Santa Clara Pueblo. Although introduced by Rose Gonzales at San Ildefonso in the 1930s, carving became a mainstay of the matriarch potters of Santa Clara as well. One of these artists, Margaret Tafoya (fig. 52), was known for the grand scale of her pottery; however, her deeply carved surfaces reflect her most exceptional skill. Another Santa Clara artist, Elizabeth Naranjo (fig. 53), is from a family of important potters. Both her work and Tafoya's give the impression of having been wrought from polished obsidian;

only when one picks them up does their relative lightness and warmth tell of their earthen origin.

William Daley and Toshiko Takaezu make large-scale sculptural pots that are all about *volume.* They come at this in very different ways. Daley takes an architectural approach to pots such as this one (fig. 54), produced as part of a series in 1986. He makes complex drawings as he works out the geometries of the pieces.[20] Daley is as interested in the interior volume as he is the exterior, and his monumental pots have the feel of ancient Incan or Mayan ritual vessels.

Takaezu works in a wide range of scales, but her larger works (and this is by no means the largest) appear to be as much about volume as about the painterly surface. The finger marks of her throwing on this piece (fig. 55) seem to have been made while trying to keep the expanding volume inside from bursting out—as if, as she created the piece, she embraced it in order to control it. Because of the tiny openings, the interior of Takaezu's pots remain mysterious.

52 *(opposite)*
MARGARET TAFOYA
SANTA CLARA PUEBLO, NM

Jar with carved decoration, 1979. Coiled and carved earthenware. Museum purchase 1979 through the Sophronia Anderson Bequest Fund (79.620). Purchased from the Mudd-Carr Gallery, Santa Fe, NM. 7.75"H x 7.75"Dia.

53
ELIZABETH NARANJO
SANTA CLARA PUEBLO, NM

Black jar with carved decoration, 1980. Coiled and carved earthenware. Purchase 1979 Sophronia Anderson Bequest Fund (79.621). Purchased from the Mudd-Carr Gallery, Santa Fe, NM. 9"H x 8.9"Dia.

Only the rattling ball of clay or pebble that she typically places inside reminds you of that unseen space.

Master potter Kimiaki Takeuchi has come to dominate the Japanese *tokoname* tradition of refined yet rough utilitarian ware, and particularly the *tsubo* or tea-storage jar (fig. 56). Unlike its ancestors, however, this piece was intended as a contemplative work, its rounded shape and subtly fire-colored surface providing the visual pleasure. In a similar way, the exaggerated volume and tiny opening of Otto and Vivika Heino's spotted orange jar (fig. 57) echo the idea of the useful vessel transformed into sculpture. As one studies the Heinos' pot one forgets any sense of utility and gets lost in the luscious glaze and the sensual swelling of the body. This is a piece one wants to caress.

A similar reaction is provoked by both Val Cushing, a longtime ceramics teacher at Alfred University (fig. 58), and his student Christopher Staley (fig. 59). These potters have taken the timeless, functional lidded vessel as inspiration. Both of them manipulate the scale and surface of the vessel, emphasize the swelling volumes within and transform a storage jar into something simultaneously unwieldy and exotically beautiful. Cushing's "acorn" vessel seems to meld rural southern American ash-glazed "turned" pots with a Japanese sense of restraint and elegance, not to mention an abstract reference to nature and fertility. Staley's jar is more gestural; the scars and rough shaping of the

54
WILLIAM DALEY
ELKINS PARK, PA

Conic Chamber, *1986. Handbuilt stoneware. Purchase 2002 Membership Endowment Fund and Felix Fuld Bequest Fund (2002.23.10). Purchased from the Garth Clark Gallery, New York City. 14"H x 28"W x 25"D.*

55 *(opposite)*
TOSHIKO TAKAEZU
QUAKERTOWN, NJ

Large closed vessel, 1983–84. Thrown and painted stoneware. Gift of Hope Yampol in memory of Jay Yampol, 1989 (89.63). 25"H x 15.6"Dia.

56
KIMIAKI TAKEUCHI
TOKONAME, JAPAN

*Tea jar (tsubo), 1980–84. Thrown
stoneware with salt glaze. Purchase
1984 Mathilde Oestrich Bequest
Fund (84.375). Purchased from
Toyobi Gallery, New York City.
11.75"H x 13.25"Dia.*

57
OTTO AND **VIVIKA HEINO**
OJAI, CA

*Ovoid vessel with spotted orange
glaze, 1986. Thrown stoneware.
Purchase 1987 Robert W. Blasberg
Memorial Fund (87.6). Purchased
from the Lee Sclar Gallery,
Morristown, NJ. 10.75"H x 16"Dia.*

58
VAL CUSHING
ALFRED, NY

*Large acorn vessel (with two lids),
1980. Thrown stoneware. Purchase
1991 Mathilde Oestrich Bequest
Fund (91.27). Purchased from a
private collection in Short Hills,
NJ. 19.5"H x 15.75"Dia.*

59
CHRISTOPHER STALEY
PROVIDENCE, RI

*Large lidded jar, 1984. Thrown
earthenware. Gift of Garth Clark
and Mark Del Vecchio, 2001
(2001.78.8a, b). 23.5"H x 18"Dia.*

elements recall the potting style of Peter Voulkos (see fig. 158). Yet both jars are very elegant: Cushing's by virtue of its deft craftsmanship and pristine sense of control in such a large piece, and Staley's with its rich coloring and voluptuous shapes. Further, Staley uses gold on his pot, much as Japanese restorers use gold lacquer to repair treasured pots.

Very early on, Richard DeVore's pots ceased to be functional and became metaphors for the human form. The large, reddish vessel from 1977 (fig. 60), of a kind sometimes referred to as "torso" vessels, is at first glance a tall, roughly cylindrical pot balanced on a small, almost invisible foot. The more one looks at it, however, the more human it becomes. It is a torso—limbless and abstract— but the sensuous contours do evoke the body, and then one begins to wonder: is that bump on the side a wart? A belly button? A nipple? Since the 1970s DeVore's work has continued to evolve in this direction, his increasingly complex—and yet distinctive—forms growing more sexual, and at times even unnerving in their suggestiveness.

Unlike his torso vessels, many of DeVore's other works are (like William Daley's) just as concerned with the interiors as with the exteriors. A work produced in late 2001 (fig. 61) addresses the terrorist attacks on the World Trade Center, which the artist witnessed while on a visit to Manhattan. The womb-like quality of the bowl is familiar from DeVore's other work, as are the sensual curves and surface textures, but there is also a sense of tension between growth and decay, evident in the scar-like diagonals and the broken edges of the upper rim (see page 1).[21] DeVore's pots are as carefully engineered as the Natzlers' early work. They are strong and stable, yet they have a look of vulnerability, as if balanced on the edge of collapse.

Three important works from the mid-1980s show how contemporary sculptural vessels may intentionally evoke traditional decorative-arts forms. This subversive interplay of art and decorative arts may elude "fine art" experts, but it is sure to win the heart of a decorative arts curator.

Betty Woodman's large vessels (fig. 62) call up images of Victorian mantel-piece garnitures or shelves of Renaissance kitchen crockery, while both Jerry Rothman and Kenneth Ferguson seem to be giving us brutal, elemental versions of dainty Victorian porcelain pieces. Woodman's wonderfully vigorous pottery jars generate images of a wide range of folk pottery, from Tang Dynasty China to Renaissance Italy to rural England. Not only does this triptych have a

60
RICHARD DEVORE
FORT COLLINS, CO

Red Torso Vessel, *1977. Handbuilt
earthenware. Purchase 1993
Decorative Arts Purchase Fund and
The Members' Fund (93.85).
Purchased from the Garth Clark
Gallery, New York City. 15.5"H x
11"W x 10"D.*

61
RICHARD DEVORE
FORT COLLINS, CO

Vessel with Interior Shelf, #1027
*(in response to 9/11/01), 2001.
Handbuilt stoneware. Collection of
the artist; courtesy of Max Protetch
Gallery, New York City. 11"H x
13"W x 10.5"D.*

different personality on each face, but the baroque forms and handles seem to suggest the dancing bodies of the eponymous princesses.

Rothman's sinister and crab-like *Low Mauve Bowl* (fig. 63) is simultaneously repellent and alluring. The luminous purple interior contrasts with the shiny black, sanded glaze of the outside; one might, perversely, be inclined to fill it with water and float gardenias in it. It is powerfully evocative of a feminine, genteel centerpiece from a Gilded Age table, yet it subverts that reference with its harsh darkness.

In the same way, Ferguson's black basket (fig. 1, page 5) is a direct reference to the delicate porcelain or glass bonbon baskets that were ubiquitous in the late Victorian parlor. The hare motif—intended, no doubt, to evoke the rangy, muscular jackrabbits of the western prairies—suggests images of Easter baskets, which were another Victorian invention. One might imagine this rough, dark, masculine piece full of white eggs, merging symbols of fertility (the rabbit) and virility (the crude, Voulkos-like gestures).

In the hands of Andrea and John Gill and of Martina and Diego Aguino, familiar, usable forms have been subtly transformed into inaccessible and mysterious objects related more to archaic rituals than to everyday life. For centuries, European "portrait" dishes were used both for decoration and for food service. Henry Varnum Poor transformed this idea with his sgraffito portrait dishes in the 1930s and '40s. Andrea Gill takes it another step (fig. 64), using

62 *(opposite)*
BETTY WOODMAN
NEW YORK, NY

Three Egyptian Princesses, *1984. Thrown earthenware with painted decoration. Purchase 2002 Membership Endowment Fund, Avis Miller Pond Bequest Fund, Nell Schoellkopf Ely Miller Memorial Fund, Estate of Clara Streissguth and Estate of Pearl Gross Lee (2002.23.6.1-.3). Purchased from the Garth Clark Gallery, New York City. 22"H (tallest); 11"W (widest); 7"D (deepest).*

63
JERRY ROTHMAN
LOS ANGELES, CA

Low Mauve Bowl, *1986. Thrown and handbuilt porcelain. Purchase 1987 Franklin Conklin, Jr., Bequest Fund and James Johnson Fund (87.105). Purchased from the Garth Clark Gallery, New York City. 8.75"H x 17.5"W x 13.5"D.*

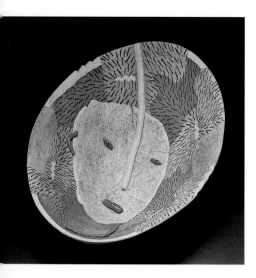

64
ANDREA GILL
ALFRED, NY

Oval bowl with blue face, late 1980s. Handbuilt earthenware with applied decoration. Gift of Vincente Lim and Robert Tooey in memory of Jay Yampol, 1991 (91.95). 5"H x 17.25"W x 12.5"D.

applied clay to create an abstracted low-relief head that could be a portrait, or even a severed head on a platter. In either case, the dish is holding the head, and one rebels at the thought of putting food on top of it.

Gill's husband John has created a painterly sculpture that is the postmodern descendant of ancient Near Eastern bird-form ewers (fig. 65). This piece is actually functional, and beautifully balanced to hold, though one might not know that to look at it. The refined clay work and exquisitely controlled glazes recall the Alfred University tradition of the "perfect pot," but Gill has put a radical spin on the idea of the functional vessel, transforming it into an elegant ritualistic object.

65
JOHN GILL
ALFRED, NY

Ewer #3, 1985. Handbuilt stoneware with applied glazes. Purchase 1986 Mathilde Oestrich Bequest Fund (86.211). Purchased from the Borgenicht Gallery, New York City. 14.5"H x 18"W x 4.5"D.

66
MARTINA AND **DIEGO AGUINO**
SAN JUAN PUEBLO, NM

Jar with incised designs, 1982.
Coiled micaceous earthenware.
Purchase 1982 The Members' Fund
(83.39). Purchased from the Letta
Wofford Gallery, Santa Fe, NM.
9.25"H x 8.25"W x 8"D.

The Aguinos, who are Native American potters, have moved from traditional vessel forms and surface treatments to pots that are distinctly postmodern in their approach. The characteristic carved mica-flecked redware vessel from the San Juan Pueblo (fig. 66) has been enhanced with a crest that might be architectural (a mission church, the adobe buildings of the pueblo) or geological (mountains or mesas). It has also evolved from being a vessel in which to store grain or water to a vessel used for ceremonial purposes only, a container for the history of the San Juan people.

Four women working with clinical precision have achieved wildly different and subversive vessels that defy function and yet celebrate the pot as a sculptural form worthy of homage. Elsa Rady's ethereal winged bowls (fig. 67) are as poised as a dancer *en pointe,* while Roseline Delisle's striped, torpedo-like vases (fig. 68) seem to spin like figure skaters. Both work in Venice, California, and they seem as far from Peter Voulkos's rough, gestural Los Angeles pots as they could be. These works are unabashedly beautiful and feminine. Oddly, these are not tactile pots; indeed Delisle's fragile engobes need to be handled with gloves to prevent finger marks. Both Rady's and Delisle's pots are the result of

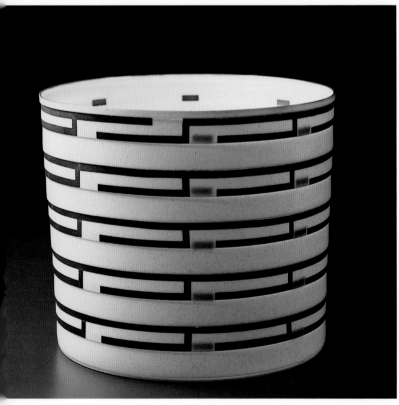

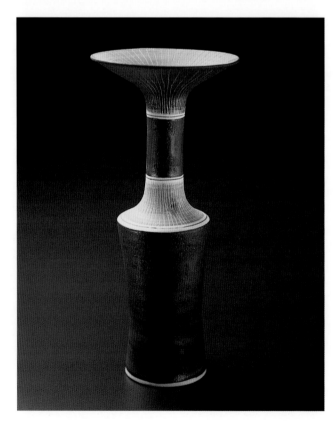

intense hands-on pottery skills, yet they demand to be appreciated from a cool, intellectual distance.

Bodil Manz, a matriarch of Danish potting, produces vessels that are solid and flat-bottomed, and yet they are made of porcelain so paper-like in its thinness and texture that the decoration on the inside is meant to be seen *through* the walls of the pot, as is apparent in this example (fig. 69). Lucie Rie's exquisite baluster vases, which are timeless in their classic form and subtle incised decoration, are so refined as to make one afraid to touch them (fig. 70). In spite of their "hands off" look, both Manz's and Rie's delicate vessels are quite tactile, and one can appreciate their beauty physically as well as visually.

SMALL WONDERS

One wouldn't know it from some of the work in this book, but big is not necessarily better. There is a human bias in favor of large scale, and a deeply ingrained sense that "big" and "important" mean the same thing. However, all of the works in this section are great pots, and all of them are very small, each piece exemplifying the best craftsmanship and aesthetic quality of its time and place.

Many of these vessels were acquired by The Newark Museum specifically *because* of their small scale. Since its founding in 1909, the museum has made a point of balancing "important" with "accessible," the masterpiece with the everyday object. Large-scale "museum" pots are fine—for museums—but most people cannot hope to own them. This museum likes to collect and exhibit objects that our visitors can look at and say, "I could live with that."

The astonishing, tiny eggshell porcelain bowl by Lucie Rie cost $7.60 at Georg Jensen in New York City in 1952 (fig. 71), but surely it is one of her most remarkable feats of throwing. It is minimalist in its aesthetic, evoking an ivory-tinted Sung Dynasty tea bowl. Porcelain is an unforgiving medium, and here Rie was paying homage to her ceramic forebears of the Western world, for

67 *(top left)*
ELSA RADY
VENICE, CA

En Deco, *1986. Thrown porcelain, enamel. Purchase 1986 Willard W. Kelsey Bequest Fund (86.212). Purchased from the Garth Clark Gallery, New York City. 6.5"H x 13.5"Dia.*

68 *(top right)*
ROSELINE DELISLE
VENICE, CA

Quintuple *(vase in five parts), 1991. Thrown porcelain with applied engobes. Purchase 1991 Sophronia Anderson Bequest Fund (91.73a–c). Purchased from the Garth Clark Gallery, New York City. 24"H x 7"Dia.*

69 *(bottom left)*
BODIL MANZ
HORVE, DENMARK

Cylindrical vessel, *1998. Slipcast porcelain with applied engobes. Museum purchase 1998 through the Members' Fund (98.70). Purchased from the Garth Clark Gallery, New York City. 7.6"H x 9.25"Dia.*

70 *(bottom right)*
LUCIE RIE
LONDON, ENGLAND

Baluster-form vase with bronze glaze, *ca. 1980. Thrown stoneware with incised decoration. Collection of Vivian and Martin Levin. 9"H x 4.4"Dia.*

whom porcelain, in its whiteness, thinness and translucency, was as precious as gold. Shoji Hamada himself would have praised the piece for its beauty and its perfectly controlled imperfection.

The equally tiny bowl by the Natzlers (fig. 72) was priced at $50 in 1949; the comparatively high price reflected, perhaps, both the superb tiger-eye glaze and the high esteem in which the Natzlers held their own work. It is an extraordinary object, technically and aesthetically, and every bit as important as any of their larger works. The thinness of the stoneware walls and the subtle, jewel-like beauty of the glaze give eloquent witness to the skill of its makers.

Because of the central role of the tea ceremony in pottery making—and because Japanese culture approaches art in an intimate, personal way—the Japanese masters have always produced important small works. Thus is it no surprise that Kjeld and Erica Deichmann, major figures in Canada's studio pottery world in the postwar years, proudly emulated the small-scale elegance and perfect craftsmanship of Japanese potters in their own work of the late 1940s. The exquisitely controlled crackled glaze of the small bowl (fig. 73), blushed with red and silky to the touch, reveal it to be an object intended as a work of art. Their small-necked vase (fig. 74) is monumental in spite of its size. The

71
LUCIE RIE
LONDON, ENGLAND

Small bowl, 1952. Thrown eggshell porcelain with clear glaze and brown rim. Purchase 1952 (52.1). Purchased from Georg Jensen, Inc., New York City. 2"H x 3.9"Dia.

72 *(opposite)*
OTTO AND GERTRUD NATZLER

LOS ANGELES, CA

Small bowl, 1948. Thrown stoneware with tiger-eye reduction glaze. Purchase 1949 (49.373). Purchased from the Van Dieman-Lilienfeld Galleries, New York City. 3.15"H x 3.75"Dia.

73
KJELD AND **ERICA**
DEICHMANN
MOSS GLEN, NEW BRUNSWICK,
CANADA

Small bowl, 1948. Thrown
stoneware with crackled glaze.
Purchase 1949 (49.365). Purchased
from the artists. 4.4"H x 4.4"Dia.

74
KJELD AND **ERICA**
DEICHMANN
MOSS GLEN, NEW BRUNSWICK,
CANADA

Small bottle vase with crackled
glaze, 1948. Thrown stoneware.
Purchase 1949 (49.366). Purchased
from the artists. 6.4"H x 3.9"Dia.

shadowy evocation of a mountain in the glaze could be a happy accident, but surely it demonstrates the intellectual and physical care that the Deichmanns lavished on this piece.

Equally monumental is the small black vessel by Hans Coper from 1966 (fig. 75). Although clearly inspired by a black-glazed Sung Dynasty cup stand, Coper has made it distinctively his own and it is every bit as powerful as his largest pieces. Coper is one of the few potters whose tiny vessels—especially those made at the end of his life—are revered by collectors. The solemn power of this small pot sets it apart.

By contrast, Allen Spencer's crisp, finely detailed lidded jar from the same year (fig. 76) is not remotely mysterious. It seems to be a perfectly functional container. However, its small scale argues against this, since it would be unable to hold a useful quantity of anything other than, say, powdered tea or a cosmetic. This little jewel is a tour de force of precisionist potting, its details as finely honed as if machine-jigged. It also seems to be in some way an homage to the eighteenth-century black basalt stoneware of Josiah Wedgwood. Spencer's jar would gain nothing by being larger, and in fact its aesthetic impact would be lessened by an increase in scale. Like Lucie Rie's little porcelain bowl, its small size makes it great.

Toshiko Takaezu's hand-sized round pots (fig. 77) are every bit as mysterious and moving as her mammoth vessels. Because they are of porcelain and not stoneware, they have a different *feel:* cooler and more delicate. They are meant to be held. Like her larger pots, this one has a rattle inside, adding a dimension of sound to that of sight and touch. Marilyn Shula's diminutive, globe-shaped pot from 1983 (fig. 78) has a similar, touchable quality. The abstract decoration with which Shula covers the curved surface appears as hieroglyphics as one holds the pot, turning it to "read" the arcane symbols.

Ruth Duckworth has worked in many scales, but some of her most moving and poetic pieces are the small white sculptural vessels that call for quiet attention (fig. 79). Unlike many small pots, Duckworth's pieces do not want to be handled; they are too white and too pure to invite one's touch, but they do demand close scrutiny. This example in particular seems like some otherworldly life-form—whether plant or animal is unclear—just emerging from an egg or a seed. If Duckworth's small white forms were larger in scale, they would lose the intimacy that makes them so powerful.

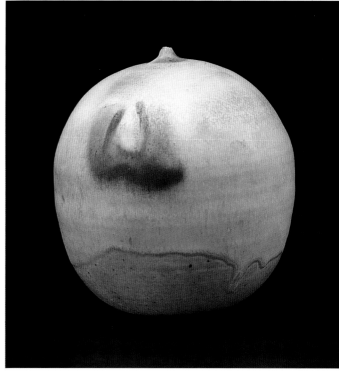

76
ALLEN SPENCER
ENGLAND

Small black covered jar, 1966.
Thrown stoneware. Purchase 1966
(66.418a, b). Purchased from Heal
& Son, Ltd., London. 4.25"H x
3.25"Dia.

75 *(opposite)*
HANS COPER
LONDON, ENGLAND

Small black vessel, 1966. Thrown
earthenware. Purchase 1966
(66.419). Purchased from Primavera
Gallery, London. 4.25"H x 3"Dia.

77
TOSHIKO TAKAEZU
CLINTON, NJ

Small closed form, 1967. Porcelain
with painted decoration. Purchase
1968 Membership Endowment
Fund (68.8). Purchased from the
artist. 5.5"H x 4.6"W x 5.25"D.

78
MARILYN SHULA
HOPI PUEBLO, AZ

*Globular pot with painted
decoration, 1983. Coiled
earthenware with applied engobes.
Purchase 1983 The Members' Fund
(83.422). Purchased from the Letta
Wofford Gallery, Santa Fe. 4.6"H x
4.75"Dia.*

79
RUTH DUCKWORTH
CHICAGO, IL

Small white vessel with winged insert, 1992. Thrown and handbuilt porcelain. Collection of Linda and Donald Schlenger. 10.5"W x 7.25"H.

80
BERNICE SUAZO NARANJO
TAOS PUEBLO, NM

Miniature weed jar with sienna color and design of bears, 1983. Coiled and carved earthenware. Purchase 1983 The Members' Fund (83.418). Purchased from the Letta Wofford Gallery, Santa Fe, NM. 1.75"H x 3.25"Dia.

81
SHOJI HAMADA
MASHIKO, JAPAN

Tea cup, 1955. Thrown stoneware with painted decoration. Purchase 1956 (56.328). Purchased from Hamada's studio in Mashiko. 3.4"H x 3.25"Dia.

82
KITAOJI ROSANJIN
YOKOHAMA, JAPAN

*Tea bowl, 1955. Thrown
earthenware with shino glaze.
Purchase 1956 (56.331). Purchased
in Tokyo. 3.5"H x 4.9"Dia.*

Bernice Naranjo has made the small form her specialty. Her grown children share her love of tiny vessels (fig. 80), and together the family has evolved into a dynasty of small-pot makers in Taos.[22] The scale of this weed jar, and its carved images of bears, give it the magical power of an amulet.

Two pieces by Japanese masters further demonstrate why small pots can be so powerful. A teacup by Hamada and a shino-glazed tea bowl by Kitaoji Rosanjin, both purchased in Japan in 1956 (figs. 81 and 82), exemplify both the calculated *mingei* roughness of Japanese tea wares and the honor paid to small scale that has so deeply impressed generations of American studio potters and collectors. Hamada's teacup is petite and minimalist, like Lucie Rie's porcelain bowl, and the simplest of brushstrokes provides vigorous calligraphic decoration. The soft facets and rich curdled glaze of Rosanjin's bowl revel in the subtle imperfections of the object's intimate form.

All of these small pots need personal contact, which sometimes makes them difficult to appreciate in the context of a museum. In the context of a home, however, they are in their element. Thus it is no surprise to find, carefully enshrined in private collections, a whole series of tea bowls by Japanese masters, or a collection of small Takaezu round forms, or a large group of small Hans Coper pots.

THE USEFUL POT

Are art and utility mutually exclusive? Michael Cardew, Bernard Leach's most famous student, thought not. Working both in England and in Africa, he spent his life making useful objects that were beautiful as well. The little rectangular baking dish Cardew made at Winchcombe, England (fig. 83), is a modest object, but its carefully crafted form and refined sense of detail belie its outwardly humble attributes. Cardew, like Leach, saw the inherent dignity and beauty in a useful pot and traditional decoration. Leach wrote about English country slipwares in *A Potter's Book,* and Cardew was himself a master reinterpreter of traditional English slip-decorated utility wares.[23]

83
MICHAEL CARDEW
WINCHCOMBE, ENGLAND

Rectangular baking dish, early 1930s. Redware with yellow glaze and black slip decoration. Gift of Garth Clark and Mark Del Vecchio, 1992 (92.49). 1.5"H x 6.9"D x 10.15"W.

84 *(opposite)*
JOHN SHELLEY
DORSET, ENGLAND

Large dish, 1959. Formed red earthenware with trailed and combed slip decoration. Purchase 1960 (60.517). Purchased from the Crafts Centre of Great Britain, London. 2.75"H x 15.75"Dia.

85
MICHAEL CARDEW
VUME, GHANA

Bowl with lily design and iridescent rust glaze, 1946. Thrown stoneware. Collection of Garth Clark and Mark Del Vecchio. 4"H x 8.5"Dia.

86 *(opposite)*
MICHAEL CARDEW
ABUJA, NIGERIA

Bowl with gray glaze, 1959–60. Thrown stoneware. Collection of Garth Clark and Mark Del Vecchio. 5.5"H x 13"Dia.

John Shelley, a Dorset potter who must have been familiar with Leach's work in St. Ives, produced a splendid charger in 1959 (fig. 84), inspired by seventeenth- and eighteenth-century English combed slipwares. Shelley capitalized on the rich graphic quality of the technique to great effect; this is peasant pottery transformed into art.

When Cardew moved to Africa, first to Vume, Ghana, in 1945, and then to Abuja, Nigeria, in 1950, he took this love of beautiful and useful pottery with him. Aside from producing his own work (figs. 85 and 86), he trained African potters to make new kinds of useful ware that suited changing needs in their communities. One of his closest associates in Ghana, Kofi Athey (fig. 87), moved to Nigeria with Cardew and worked with him at a new pottery in Abuja, which still exists today. Athey's covered casserole is a glorious mélange of cultural associations, combining Gwari influences from his native Ghana with the forms and techniques taught to him by his English mentor. A similar mixture of aesthetic attributes is evident in a small pitcher of European form by Tanko Ashada (fig. 88) and a large mug by the celebrated Ladi Kwali (fig. 89). These European forms—decorated with African motifs and techniques—were glazed

87
KOFI ATHEY
ABUJA, NIGERIA

Gwari-style covered casserole, ca.
1959. Thrown stoneware with
incised decoration. Gift of Garth
Clark and Mark Del Vecchio,
2001 (2001.78.3a, b). 5.75"H x
10.5"W x 8"D.

88
TANKO ASHADA
ABUJA, NIGERIA

Small pitcher, ca. 1960. Thrown stoneware with incising. Gift of Garth Clark and Mark Del Vecchio, 2001 (2001.78.1). 6.25"H x 5.25"W x 6"D.

89
LADI KWALI
ABUJA, NIGERIA

Large mug, ca. 1961. Thrown stoneware with incising. Gift of Garth Clark and Mark Del Vecchio, 2001 (2001.78.4). 6.25"H x 5.25"W x 3.5"D.

with rich temmoku-style glazes, an aesthetic passed on to Cardew by Bernard Leach, who would have been inspired, in turn, by his Japanese colleague Hamada. Each piece, however humble, would have ennobled any daily use to which it was put.

OPEN VESSELS

Although bowls and plates are the most common "useful" forms of studio pottery, it is difficult—especially with a piece bought initially by a museum and thus having no domestic history—to determine whether or not the object was intended for use or purely for display.

The crisp, rhythmic incised design on a 1948 bowl by the Scheiers (fig. 90) evokes Picasso's monumental painting *Guernica* of 1937. Such striking and unique graphic work was a specialty of Ed Scheier in the late 1940s, and while it makes this modest-sized bowl a powerful object,[24] it in no way lessens its functionality as a bowl. Both in shape and in scale this masterful piece seems intended for domestic use, and was purchased as such by The Newark Museum.

The same is true with Gutte Eriksen's 1955 redware bowl (fig. 91). The Scandinavians have a long tradition of investing useful wares with carefully considered craft and art. Eriksen, a major figure in postwar Danish ceramics, studied with Bernard Leach. This piece, but for its Japanese sense of scale and form, has a Scandinavian quality about it, derived from the impressed decoration and the milky blue-and-white glaze. Certainly Eriksen had no intention that this bowl would be placed on a shelf and never used. But she also was every inch the artist in her careful consideration of the flow of the glaze, the placement of the stamped design and the subtle reshaping of the thrown bowl from its original circular form.

Ronald Cooper's chop plate from 1960 (fig. 92) parallels the sort of sgraffito done by his American peers the Scheiers; pots from both studios echoed

90
EDWIN AND MARY
SCHEIER
DURHAM, NH

Brown bowl with abstract decoration, 1948. Thrown stoneware with sgraffito. Purchase 1949 Special Purchase Fund (49.371). Purchased from the artists. 5.9"H x 8"Dia.

110

91
GUTTE ERIKSEN
ST. KARLSMINDE, DENMARK

*Bowl with stamped decoration,
1955. Thrown and altered red
earthenware with blue and white
glazes. Purchase 1956 John B.
Morris Fund (56.131). Purchased
from Den Permanente,
Copenhagen. 3.6"H x 7"W x 7.5"D.*

92
RONALD C. COOPER
MIDDLESEX, ENGLAND

*Large plate with design of fish,
1960. Earthenware with olive green
slip glaze and sgraffito. Purchase
1960 (60.519). Purchased at the
Crafts Centre of Great Britain.
1.1"H x 12.25"Dia.*

the graphic works on paper characteristic of the 1950s and 1960s. In particular, the pictographic works of painter Adolph Gottlieb come to mind, although Cooper's iconography is probably less mystical than Gottlieb's and more about the food that might be served on his plate.

Bernard Leach and Shoji Hamada's visit to the United States in 1953 was a catalyst for many American potters, including Peter Voulkos, however different the direction he subsequently took. Two bowls by Leach and Hamada represent the almost prayerful respect for traditional ceramic techniques and forms—especially those of Japan—that permeated American ceramic studios in the 1950s. The Hamada bowl (fig. 93) was purchased in New York at a Japanese craft gallery called *Kogei* (Japanese for "craft") in 1952. It is an archetypal form from his studio, with its Japanese calligraphy and soft, creamy glazes. Leach's bowl (fig. 94), also purchased in New York, is a reinterpretation of a Sung form, with an odd little floral motif at its center. It is easy to see both of these bowls used to make a dinner more elegant and ceremonial. While either would be worthy of contemplation, neither would be diminished by being used to serve food.

One must remember that all of the pieces shown in this section were acquired by The Newark Museum as examples of serving pieces. Helen Pincombe's dark, muted chop plate of 1966 (fig. 95) seems to echo Scandinavian tableware produced by firms such as Finland's Arabia during that decade. Its crisp, machine-like form brings it in line with commercially produced dishes, while the subtle, wing-like shapes in the glaze mark it as an artist's work. Gillian Lowndes's deeply rimmed dish of the same year (fig. 96) veers in the other direction, its rough crystalline glaze militating against real function. Bawa Ushafa's wonderful incised charger from the beginning of the 1960s (fig. 97) is redolent of that heady mixture of Africa, England and Japan so characteristic of the Abuja pottery of that period. Obviously meant to hold a banquet's worth of food, when empty, Ushafa's plate looks like a warrior's shield.

The serene, painterly quality of Toshiko Takaezu's sculptural work is present in the abstract designs of her 1971 plate (fig. 178, page 204). Although this work is clearly a painting that can be read as a landscape or simply as an abstraction, it is also a dish on which to pile cookies or place a cake. Even today, though her own work is sculptural, Takaezu honors functionality as a goal for the artist potter.

93
SHOJI HAMADA
MASHIKO, JAPAN

Low bowl, 1952. Thrown
stoneware with calligraphic
decoration. Purchase 1952 (52.76).
Purchased from Kogei Gallery,
New York City. 2.75"H x 8.75"Dia.

94
BERNARD LEACH
ST. IVES, ENGLAND

Conical bowl, 1959. Thrown
stoneware with painted brown
decoration. Purchase 1960
(60.483). Purchased from
Bonnier's, New York City.
2.9"H x 9.5"Dia.

95
HELEN PINCOMBE
ENGLAND

Plate, 1966. Thrown stoneware with painted decoration. Purchase 1966 (66.416). Purchased from Primavera Gallery, London. 1.25"H x 12.5"Dia.

96
GILLIAN LOWNDES
ENGLAND

Deep plate, 1966. Thrown earthenware with crystalline glaze. Purchase 1966 (66.428). Purchased from Primavera Gallery, London. 2.75"H x 13"Dia.

97 *(opposite)*
BAWA USHAFA
ABUJA, NIGERIA

Large plate, ca. 1961. Thrown stoneware with incising. Gift of Garth Clark and Mark Del Vecchio, 2001 (2001.78.2). 2"H x 14.25"Dia.

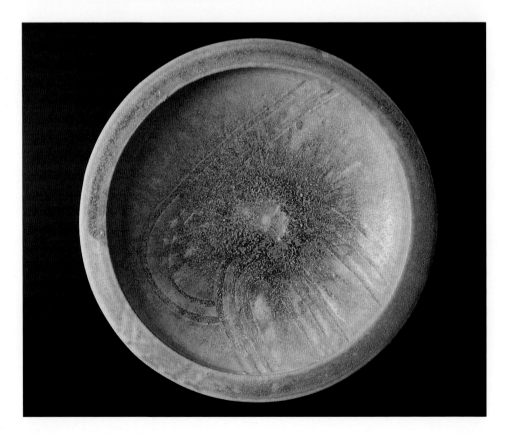

98
BETTY WOODMAN
NEW YORK, NY

Oval cake stand, 1983. Handbuilt earthenware with applied glazes. Gift of Garth Clark and Mark Del Vecchio, 1991 (91.108). 5.4"H x 16.75"W x 9.25"D.

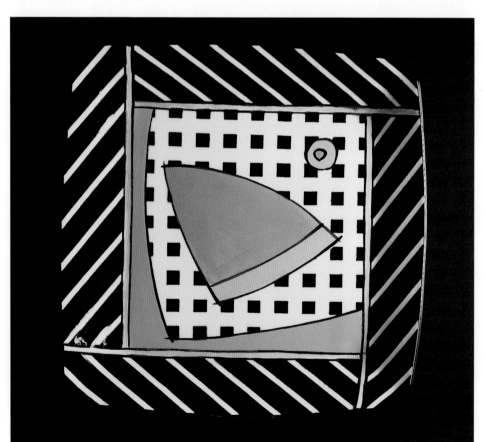

99
DOROTHY HAFNER
NEW YORK, NY

Pink Triangle *square platter or chop plate, 1989. White earthenware with applied glazes. Purchase 1989 Estate of Pearl Gross Lee (89.28). Purchased from the artist. 1"H x 12.4"W x 12.25"D.*

118

The mood of the 1980s is clear in Betty Woodman's well-known use of majolica colors and freely painted decoration in her cake stand (fig. 98).[25] Influenced by the artist's life in Italy, this piece is vigorous and cheerful, with an earthy peasant quality that speaks of European folk pottery. It speaks, too, of plentiful dinner parties with great crusty loaves of bread, rich rum-soaked cakes and flasks of hearty local red wine. Yet for all its friendly utility, the stand is nonetheless a piece of sculpture, and the hand and artistic intent of the maker are evident.

In a rather different manifestation of 1980s conviviality, Dorothy Hafner created a successful enterprise producing her stylish, colorful, carefully made tablewares (fig. 99). Her bright, pop-graphic designs stand, like Woodman's, in strong contrast to the subtler, more self-consciously restrained aesthetic of an earlier generation.

VASES AND BOTTLES

The vase is a key form of the useful vessel, and its evolution is apparent across the decades. Each of the vases shown here, in spite of varying degrees of sculptural quality, would readily lend itself to its purported function. Of course vases have always been used as purely contemplative objects in Asia, as well as in the West, because every vase's primary purpose is decorative: to hold flowers or foliage.

Among the rarest forms produced by the German-English potter Hans Coper, his "tripots" of the late 1950s were, perhaps more than any other of his forms, very *fifties*-looking. The tapered cylindrical forms and asymmetrical grouping are iconic design motifs of that decade.[26] This magnificent example of that form (fig. 100) is both completely sculptural in its stance and totally useful as a weed pot. The form, for all its "retro" aspect, seems to be derived from Chinese double vases of the eighteenth century (and probably earlier). The three vessels of differing heights suggest the Japanese use of three heights of

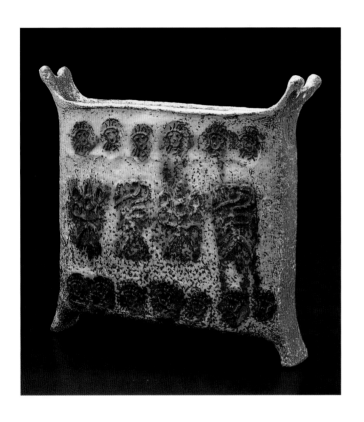

101
YIEN KOO WANG (KING)
NEW YORK, NY

*Flower vessel, 1959. Handbuilt
stoneware with relief decoration.
Purchase 1960 (60.512). Purchased
from the artist. 12"H x 12"W x 3"D.*

100 *(opposite)*
HANS COPER
LONDON, ENGLAND

*Tripot vase, 1958. Thrown
stoneware. Purchase 1959 (59.23).
Purchased from Bonnier's, New
York City. 14"H x 8"W x 8.25"D.*

102
GORDON CROSBY
WIMBLEDON, ENGLAND

*Vase, 1965. Handbuilt stoneware.
Purchase 1966 (66.52). Purchased
from Primavera Gallery, London.
7.25"H x 10.4"W x 3.5"D.*

flowers or foliage in the classic flower-arranging art known as *ikebana*. It's hard to imagine that Coper wasn't aware of this.

Yien Koo Wang, daughter of celebrated Chinese painter C.C. Wang, consciously echoes an archaic Chinese bronze in her slab-built flower vessel of 1959 (fig. 101). The colors of her glazes evoke the patinated and corroded surfaces of long-buried metal, and the runic symbols that adorn the sides of her vase recall the inscribed terra-cotta "envelopes" that held cuneiform tablets millennia ago. But such rectangular flower holders have their roots in the seventeenth- and eighteenth-century tin-glazed flower bricks of England and Holland, as well. Just a few strands of wheat or tall dried flowers could fit in the small, off-center opening of Gordon Crosby's slab-built vase (fig. 102), which reflects the sharp angularity of British architecture and furniture from the mid-1960s. Softer and more evocative of traditional slab-molded Japanese bottle vases is Belgian potter Pierre Culot's version from the same period (fig. 103). Both of these vases, purchased in London in 1966, demonstrate the functional mode of northern European pottery making at that time, still prevalent in spite of the radical shifts in ceramic art developing on the academic front in the United States.

103 *(opposite)*
PIERRE CULOT
ROUX-MIROIR, BELGIUM

Slab bottle vase, 1965–66. Handbuilt stoneware, painted decoration. Purchase 1966 (66.429). Purchased from Primavera Gallery, London. 11"H x 9.5"W x 4.25"D.

104 *(bottom left)*
LUCIE RIE
LONDON, ENGLAND

Thrown vase of pink and blue stoneware, 1980s. Gift of Alice and Malcolm Nanes, 2001 (2001.57.2). 7.5"H x 3.25"W x 2.35"D.

105 *(bottom right)*
JEFFREY OESTREICH
TAYLOR'S FALLS, MN

Faceted vase with temmoku glaze, 1983. Thrown stoneware. Gift of Irma and Larry Starr, 1991 (91.12). 14"H x 7.75"W x 7.25"D.

Lucie Rie's little pink and blue vase from around 1980 (fig. 104) shows a technical breakthrough that allowed Rie to throw with combined colored clays. This was an unusual color scheme in her oeuvre, and unlike many of her colder, more brittle-looking works, this is a tactile vessel whose bubbled texture and nursery color scheme invite holding. Jeff Oestreich, a student of Warren MacKenzie, the American heir to Bernard Leach's traditional approach, offers an elegant, classic Japanese vase (fig. 105), richly faceted and elegantly dressed in glossy temmoku. Whether placed empty in a spotlit niche or full of dahlias on a kitchen table—either way this great traditionalist vase would shine.

COVERED VESSELS

Derived from forms dating to prehistory, covered food storage and service vessels of all varieties have been explored by contemporary studio potters. In 1952, The Newark Museum's curator of Asian Art, Eleanor Olson, purchased a little

106
SHOJI HAMADA
MASHIKO, JAPAN

Soup bowl with lid, 1946–51. Thrown stoneware with gray glaze. Purchase 1952 (52.74). Purchased from Kogei Gallery, New York City. Bowl: 2.5"H; lid: 4.5"Dia.

107 *(opposite)*
PETER VOULKOS
HELENA, MT

Covered jar with flattened sides, 1952. Thrown stoneware with wax-resist decoration. Purchase 1987 Willard W. Kelsey Bequest Fund (87.8a, b). Purchased from the Garth Clark Gallery, New York City. 15.75"H x 11.25"W x 11.25"D.

108
LUCIE RIE
LONDON, ENGLAND

Cigarette box, 1959. Thrown stoneware with sgraffito. Purchase 1960 (60.559). Purchased at Heal & Son, Ltd., London. 3.6"H x 2"Dia.

109
BERNICE SUAZO NARANJO
TAOS PUEBLO, NM

Bean pot of micaceous clay, 1983. Coiled and incised earthenware. Purchase 1983 The Members' Fund (83.420a, b). Purchased from the Letta Wofford Gallery, Santa Fe, NM. 5.15"H x 8.6"Dia.

covered soup dish from Kogei, a Japanese craft gallery in New York. The piece (fig. 106) was made by Shoji Hamada, a potter in Occupied Japan. The curator, who was thinking ethnologically, knew little of Hamada and nothing of his relationship with Bernard Leach. She may have known that Hamada was an important figure in Japanese pottery, but probably did not suspect that he was conversant with English folk pottery or that, with Leach, he was about to embark upon a trip that would change the face of American studio ceramics. What this curator did understand was that Hamada produced everyday, useful pots with a careful eye to detail and craftsmanship. In his hands, even the humblest vessel became something worthy of respect.

At this same moment, Peter Voulkos was winning prizes with his covered vessels in Montana, long before he started his Los Angeles ceramics revolution. Voulkos did his master's thesis on the lidded jar,[27] and this "cookie jar" (fig. 107), originally owned by the California pop painter Wayne Thiebaud, is one of his finest early pieces. The wax-resist decoration on the flattened sides of this jar once again recalls the calligraphic images of Adolph Gottlieb and other mid-twentieth-century abstractionists.

Lucie Rie, with her diminutive, minimalist cylindrical cigarette box from 1959 (fig. 108), demonstrates her roots in Austrian modernist design,[28] while also proving that a small object can have a powerful artistic presence. When The Newark Museum's first decorative arts curator, Margaret White, purchased this piece at Heal & Son in London, it was because she recognized the extraordinary care that Rie had invested in a utilitarian object. As formidable a presence as Rie was in English ceramics, she was happy to lavish the same attention on a small (and undoubtedly low-profit) piece as she did on her most "important" and costly vessels.

The same kind of minimalist incised lines with which Rie ornamented her work appear in a strikingly different context in the 1983 bean pot by Taos potter Bernice Suazo Naranjo (fig. 109). Naranjo, known for her careful, shallow pictorial carving, took a traditional Taos container for cooking *frijoles* and updated it in a dramatically austere way. The micaceous clay is scarred with many random lines, and the flat, slightly conical lid has a central hole, allowing steam to escape while also serving as a finger hold. The lid seems to invoke the idea of a volcano, and the pot seems at once ancient and modern. The artist has given this serving vessel a distinct late-twentieth-century presence.

Kit-Yin Snyder, born in Canton, has long abandoned ceramics for sculpture and video, but back in the mid-1960s she paid homage to her Asian roots, invoking tea-storage vessels in contemporary guise (fig. 110). The building technique she uses here suggests folded paper construction, and the subtle play of the red body and the uneven shino glaze changes with every side. In a like manner, Karen Karnes's paired jars from 1968 (fig. 111) are not identical, thus creating a visual dialogue between them that goes beyond mere function. The absence of either jar diminishes the aesthetic experience of the whole. In this way Karnes anticipates Betty Woodman's triptych of the early 1980s (fig. 62).

Even though Mizuki Yoshikawa's sleek black-glazed box from the late 1970s (fig. 112) refers directly to early Japanese lacquered food boxes, its minimalist form parallels the minimalist conceptual sculpture of Donald Judd. However, instead of holding the uninitiated at arm's length as Judd's work does, Yoshikawa's box, because of its small scale and accessible domesticity, invites a closer exploration and an intimate aesthetic experience when the contrasting decorated interior is revealed. Yoshikawa's work shares this sense of intimacy with the works of Snyder and Karnes.

TEMPEST IN A TEAPOT

Even though tea drinking in America has long been overshadowed by coffee drinking, it is the teapot that is the most beloved and enduring of functional forms, explored and re-explored by studio potters. Perhaps the coffeepot hasn't the same psychic power, but it is more likely that coffee drinkers, since the 1920s, have been focused on electronic gadgets such as percolators, grinders and brewing machines. Tea-making continues to be a manual, meditative process, and thus the teapot survives conceptually as a contemplative functional form.

When Richard Kjaergaard, a Danish potter, produced his tooled redware pots (fig. 113) in the 1950s, he was combining modern Scandinavian design with red Yixing stoneware in a modernist, biomorphic homage to an ancient Chinese tradition.[29] At the same time in England, Lucie Rie was infusing her well-known side-handled coffeepots (fig. 114) with a sleek modernism that ran

114
LUCIE RIE
LONDON, ENGLAND

Coffeepot with side handle, 1954.
Thrown stoneware with black glaze
and incised lines. Collection of
Linda and Donald Schlenger. 9"H
x 9"W x 5"D.

115
BYRON TEMPLE
LAMBERTVILLE, NJ

Teapot with metal handle, 1987.
Thrown salt-glazed porcelain. Gift
of Sandra and Louis Grotta, 1991
(91.40a, b). 7.5"H x 5.75"W x
4.25"D.

113 *(opposite)*
RICHARD KJAERGAARD
COPENHAGEN, DENMARK

Teapot with tooled surface, 1955.
Thrown red stoneware, rattan.
Purchase 1956 John B. Morris
Fund (56.133a, b). Purchased from
Den Permanente, Copenhagen. 5"H
x 7.5"W x 5.5"D.

counter to the rustic folk aesthetic of the Leach-Hamada school. A generation later, New Jersey's leading traditionalist, Byron Temple, produced an elegant, intelligent *mingei* teapot of salt-glazed porcelain (fig. 115). Temple's adherence to unpretentious functional forms and modest scale gives evidence of his apprenticeship with Bernard Leach in the late 1950s.

In another generation's remixing of that same tradition, Stephen Fabrico produced a 1990 teapot (fig. 116) that is a postmodern melding of Japanese forms (the handle and lid), art deco revisionism and Native American blackware revivalism. At the same time that Fabrico made his intentionally slick, polished teapot, New York–based Ragner Naess (fig. 117) combined postmodernist geometry (spheres made a huge comeback in the 1980s) with a neo-archaic, Asian utilitarianism. Basic materials and simple decoration signaled a true tea lover's teapot. Simultaneously, Jeff Oestreich, who carries on the *mingei* tradition in Minnesota through his training with Warren MacKenzie, was creating his distinctive, subtle take on the Asian teapot. In this instance (fig. 118), he has rendered it startling by means of an unusual and delicious green glaze.[30]

Bruce Winn's 1994 faceted teapot (fig. 119) revels in the same postmodern embrace of pattern and color that marks the work of Ralph Bacerra and Dorothy Hafner. All of these 1990s teapots are notable also for their relatively large size—a direct contrast to the petite scale of traditional Asian teapots.[31] Mark Shapiro, a New England traditionalist, has reduced the size of his recent teapots (fig. 120), making them feel more intimate and private—and hence more Asian.

The nonfunctional teapot continues to be an inspiration to contemporary studio potters, who often move from function to fantasy in their own development of the form. All but one of the teapots in this section could function (if one tried hard enough), but clearly they deal with the *concept,* rather than the *use,* of a teapot.

Richard Notkin's extraordinary small-scale teapots of the mid-1980s were directly inspired by the little stoneware teapots from the Yixing kilns in China—one of the few Chinese pottery traditions in which individual artists have emerged. Notkin's *Curbside Teapot* of 1986 (fig. 121) is both whimsical and dark. Its scale requires one to look closely, and to marvel at the artist's sculptural detail. Such close study, however, raises the issues of pollution and urban decay—and brings to mind the question of where the water for our tea actually

116
STEPHEN FABRICO
BLOOMINGTON, NY

Fluted black teapot, 1990.
Porcelain. Gift of Diana Sobo
Gast, 1990 (90.252a, b). 11"H x
10.5"W x 7.25"D.

117
RAGNER NAESS
BROOKLYN, NY

Teapot and warmer, 1990. Thrown
and incised earthenware. Gift of
Hilde Siegel, 1990 (90.235a–c).
Teapot and warmer: 11"H (overall)
x 10.25"W x 6.5"D.

118 *(opposite)*
JEFFREY OESTREICH
TAYLOR'S FALLS, MN

Teapot with bright green glaze, 1990. Handbuilt stoneware. Purchase 1990 Alice W. Kendall Bequest Fund (90.239a, b). Purchased from The Works Gallery, Philadelphia. 7.5"H x 12"W x 4.75"D.

119
BRUCE WINN
JERSEY CITY, NJ

Teapot, 1994. Thrown and altered stoneware with colored glazes. Purchase 1994 Emma Fantone Endowment for Decorative Arts (94.47a, b). Purchased from the artist from an exhibition at The Newark Museum. 6.5"H x 13.5"W x 7.5"D.

120
MARK SHAPIRO
WORTHINGTON, MA

Teapot with faceted body, 2002. Thrown and altered stoneware with black glaze. Gift of Vicky and Richard McGlynn, 2002 (2002.20a, b). 7.5"H x 8"W x 6.5"D.

135

122
DING FANG ZHOU
YIXING, CHINA

On the Edge, *1998. Handbuilt
stoneware. Gift of Louise and
James Anderson, 2001 (2001.80.2a,
b). 5.75"H x 11"W x 3.4"D.*

comes from. Contemporary Yixing master potter Ding Fang Zhou (fig. 122) contents himself with a more formalist approach, creating an illusionistic interplay of texture and color with no sinister overtones. The rebelliousness here is in the artist's casting off of the historical limitations of Yixing wares (i.e., function) to allow himself the luxury of exploring the sculptural possibilities of his format. Wen Xia and Jian Xing Lu—who, like Zhou, are Chinese—produce a piece that is even more whimsical (fig. 123), making bamboo do impossible things, while at the same time showing off their consummate skills at depicting botanical detail within a balanced form.[32]

If Annette Corcoran's immediately recognizable bird-form teapots (fig. 124) had their origin in the same ancient Near Eastern bird-form ewers that inspired John Gill (fig. 65), her work has begun to leave that historical avatar behind.[33] The presence of a spout, lid and handle on her *Montagu's Harrier* of 2000 seem at first glance to be merely design challenges with no deeper purpose. The realism of the carefully painted details, however, contrasts with the stylized drawing on the bird's back, which shows a bird in flight (see page 27). There at first seems to be some intentional connection with Native American imagery. However, the bird itself is in fact native not to the United States but

121 *(opposite)*
RICHARD NOTKIN
MYRTLE POINT, OR

Curbside Teapot, *1986. Cast and
carved stoneware. Purchase 1987
Willard W. Kelsey Bequest Fund
(87.7a, b). Purchased from the
Garth Clark Gallery, New York
City. 5"H x 7.75"W x 4"D.*

123
WEN XIA LU AND JIAN XING LU
YIXING, CHINA

Dancing Bamboo, *2000.*
Handbuilt stoneware. Gift of
Louise and James Anderson, 2001
(2001.80.1a, b). 11"H x 9.5"W x
3.4"D.

124 *(opposite)*
ANNETTE CORCORAN
PACIFIC GROVE, CA

Montagu's Harrier, *2000. Painted*
porcelain. Purchase 2002 Friends of
Decorative Arts Fund (2002.9.2a,
b). Purchased from the Leslie
Ferrin Gallery, Croton-on-
Hudson, NY. 12"H x 6"W x 5.25"D.

to Europe, where it summers after migrating from winter quarters in sub-Saharan Africa and Asia. In Europe it has become rare and in England nearly extinct because of human inroads on its habitat. Thus the connection is made between the bird and the two dominant tea-drinking populations (in China and England), where it struggles to keep a foothold in the modern world.

Eunjung Park, on the other hand, takes another route in exploring the sculptural possibilities of the teapot (fig. 125). The Korean-born and -educated potter, who got her M.F.A. at the Rhode Island School of Design, combines the vegetable forms of Yixing stoneware teapots with the china-painting tradition of the nineteenth century to create a personal vision—indeed, a worm's-eye landscape—of her native country. The flora and fauna of this teapot and stand (which is functional once you figure out where things go) are native to Korea. Her naturalistically colored porcelain body, however, seems more to evoke the European tradition of illusionistic tablewares, particularly those of English pottery and porcelain in the eighteenth century.

125
EUNJUNG PARK
PROVIDENCE, RI

Korean Landscape II, *2000.*
Handbuilt and china-painted
porcelain. Purchase 2002 Friends of
Decorative Arts Fund (2002.9.3a,
b). Purchased from the Leslie
Ferrin Gallery, Croton-on-Hudson,
NY. 7"H x 14.25"W x 4.15"D.

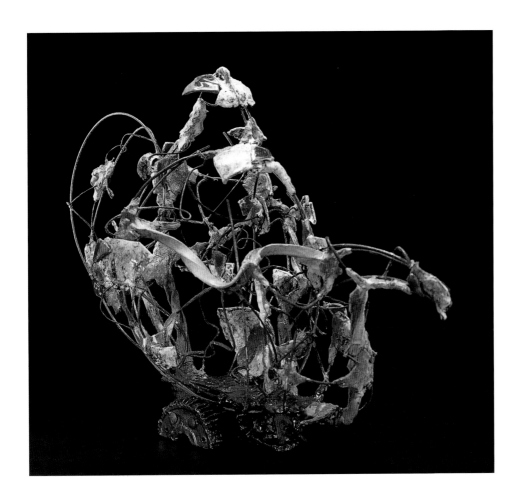

126
RAYMON ELOZUA
NEW YORK, NY

Wireframe Teapot #1, *1993.*
Glazed ceramic on wire armature.
Promised gift of Patricia Feiwel in
memory of Henry Feiwel, 2002
(TR39.2002). 23"H x 33"W x 17"D.

One might note that while each of these pieces has a title, only two incorporate the word "teapot," and one of these is the furthest removed from a traditional teapot form. The ultimate *concept* of a teapot—in physical form—can be seen in the eerie and alluring sculptures of Raymon Elozua (fig. 126). Elozua has deconstructed the teapot into a haunting ghost of a vessel, enlarged in scale and exploded into a wire armature spattered with brightly colored fragments of clay. His postindustrialist vision of the teapot is dark and frightening, and yet even here the artist revels in the teapot's traditional form and in the colors and surfaces achievable with ceramics.

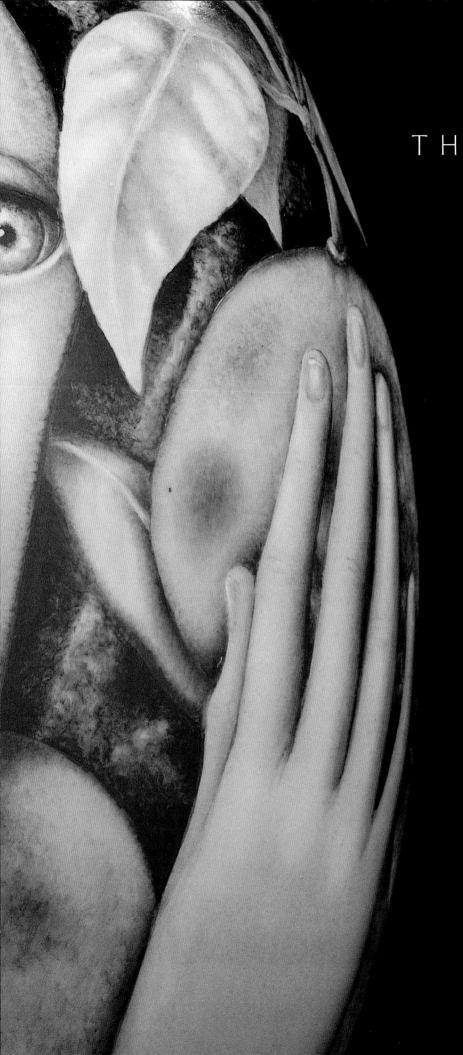

TH

THE NARRATIVE POT

The narrative pot is a pot that, quite simply, tells a story. Although narrative decoration has always been part of pottery making (ancient Greek pots and sixteenth-century Italian *maiolica* are two important traditions), it has taken on a distinctive character in the hands of contemporary studio potters.

Take a look at the Scheiers' large plate from 1948 (fig. 127), which depicts the biblical story of the judgment of Solomon. Although popular in Renaissance Italy, biblical themes are unusual in the studio pottery of the late 1940s.[34] By placing the figures of the baby and the two mothers inside the space of the wise king's head, Ed Scheier manages to telegraph the idea that it was in Solomon's *head,* in his imagination, that the drama was played out. One could ostensibly use this platter for serving food but, as with Andrea Gill's oval bowl with a blue face (see fig. 64), it would seem like desecration to do so.

127 *(opposite)*
EDWIN and **MARY SCHEIER**
DURHAM, NH

Judgment of Solomon *plate, 1948. Red stoneware with painted decoration. Purchase 1949 Special Purchase Fund (49.370). Purchased from the artists. 0.8"H x 14.5"Dia.*

128
RICHARD NOTKIN
MYRTLE POINT, OR

Celadon Cooling Towers Teapot, *1983. Cast and carved porcelain. Gift of Larry and Sandra Zellner, 1991 (91.26a, b). 6.4"H x 9.25"W x 3.75"D.*

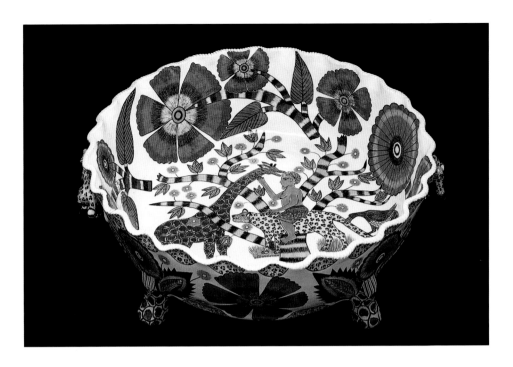

130
BONNIE NTSHALINTSHALI
WINSTON, SOUTH AFRICA

*Footed bowl, 1995. Thrown and
handbuilt white earthenware with
painted decoration. Purchase 1996
Louis Bamberger Bequest Fund
(96.32). Purchased from the
Ardmore Ceramic Art Studio,
Winterton, South Africa. 5.5"H x
17"Dia.*

Richard Notkin's delicate *Celadon Cooling Towers Teapot* of 1983 (fig. 128) is an example of a narrative *sculptural* pot. This work was certainly inspired by the Three Mile Island disaster, but it more generally tells a clear and chilling story of the quest for electricity through nuclear technology, as well as the ultimate threat of nuclear disaster and death. Notkin has cleverly derived his form from the Yixing tradition of the conjoined double-vessel teapot.

Anne Kraus makes masterful use of underglazing in her narrative imagery. Her delicate drawings, carefully thought out shapes and beautiful sense of color complement the narratives that unreel as you study her pots. In contrast to the public and mythical narratives of the Scheier and Notkin pieces, Kraus's narratives are personal, timeless and dream-like. The *Endurance* bowl (fig. 129) is both personal and generalized: it speaks of the problems encountered by artists trying to make their way in the world.

Compare Kraus's work with the large painted bowl by Zulu potter Bonnie Ntshalintshali (fig. 130) from 1995. Ntshalintshali (who died at 32 in 1999) was a self-taught artist and potter, and her child-like style suited the themes of her pots and sculptural pieces. Her narratives were often derived from Bible stories learned at her childhood mission school, and were placed, of course, in the context of southern Africa's unique natural setting, replete with wild animals and exotic plants and flowers.

129 *(opposite)*
ANNE KRAUS
SHORT HILLS, NJ

Endurance *bowl, 1985. Slipcast
white stoneware with applied
glazes. Purchase 1985 John C.
Williams Bequest Fund (85.225).
Purchased from the Garth Clark
Gallery, New York City. 2.75"H x
12"Dia.*

Nathan Begay, a Hopi potter, brings a Native American narrative tradition to his 1980 pot *Rainbirds, Coming Storm* (fig. 131). The vast landscape of Arizona is suggested, with mountains stretching across the horizon, while stylized geometric birds flee before storm clouds and torrential rain. Here, instead of personalized meaning, the artist draws upon timeless symbolism at the core of his people's way of life.

Akio Takamori is known for large-scale handbuilt vessels that are, in essence, three-dimensional figure drawings; these works rely on ivory-colored clay and bold black outlining detailed in iron red (fig. 132). This piece, titled *Mythology*, was inspired by the dramatic shift in the artist's life when he married and became a father. On one side (not shown) the viewer sees him as the anxious father, reading the myth of Laocoön, who was killed trying to rescue his sons. On the other side he looks on in bemused adoration at his wife and infant child. He is a proud father, yet he is also alienated, pushed away by the unique bond between mother and child that he cannot share.

Completely different in character is Anne Kraus's *Kiln Bowl* of 1984 (fig. 133). This is possibly the first piece of decorated whiteware Kraus made in her new studio in the basement of her parents' house in Short Hills, New Jersey,

131
NATHAN BEGAY
HOPI PUEBLO, AZ

Rainbirds, Coming Storm, *1980–83. Jar with painted decoration, 1980–83. Coiled earthenware with applied engobes. Purchase 1983 The Members' Fund (83.421). Purchased from the Letta Wofford Gallery, Santa Fe, NM. 5.5"H x 7.5"Dia.*

132 *(opposite)*
AKIO TAKAMORI
SEATTLE, WA

Mythology, *1994. Handbuilt stoneware with painted decoration. Collection of Linda and Donald Schlenger. 25"H x 29"W.*

after graduating from Alfred University. The narrative decoration for which she is best known had not yet fully developed, and this bowl shows gray, undecorated vessels, with her kiln sitting forlornly (and expectantly) in the middle of the room.

Narrative need not be explicit: it can be referential or suggestive. Michael Lucero's spectacular, flamboyant sculptures take their narrative cues from the entire world of art history. His 1992 *Head with Ohr Top* (fig. 134) is not a linear narrative, but rather a surreal incantation that calls up thousands of years of ceramic history. Pitchers and jugs modeled on human heads were produced as popular domestic ceramics in Roman times and have reappeared sporadically ever since,[35] but it is the American vernacular variation to which Lucero's work refers. In rural southern America, head jugs have evolved from a utilitarian form to a folk-sculptural form, often being produced by several generations within a single family. Lucero's pot pays homage broadly to indigenous rural folk art. At the same time, the crumpled and glazed opening at the top of his jug tips a hat to another southern art pottery master, George Ohr. This remarkable turn-of-the-century potter from Biloxi, Mississippi, was one of the first studio potters in America.[36]

133
ANNE KRAUS
SHORT HILLS, NJ

Kiln Bowl, *1984. Slipcast white earthenware with applied glazes. Purchase 1999 Parker O. Griffith Bequest Fund and Membership Endowment Fund and partial gift of Garth Clark and Mark Del Vecchio, 1999 (99.87). 2.25"H x 12.6"W x 11.5"D.*

150

134
MICHAEL LUCERO
NEW YORK, NY

Head with Ohr Top, *1992.*
Stoneware with colored glazes.
Collection of Linda and Donald
Schlenger. 17"H x 14"Dia.

Kurt Weiser's china-painted porcelain pots are sensual and suggestive (fig. 135). A splendid technician, Weiser takes the nineteenth-century, genteel china-painting tradition (which was both male and female, professional and amateur) and turns it on its head. His large-scale pots, rather like warped Chinese ginger jars, become curved canvases for his lush, colorful jungles and otherworldly, androgynous people. Here, as with Lucero, his narratives are nonspecific, seeming often to refer to some slightly sinister Eden. The carefully detailed fruit, insects and birds have a nightmarish aspect that places them in the realm of the mind, rather than anywhere in the actual world.

This nightmarish quality is certainly present in the work of Grayson Perry, an English potter who has moved as far from the world of Bernard Leach as is humanly possible. Perry's *Essex Man* of 1999 (fig. 136) specifically references the work of Edward Bingham, a quasi-folk, quasi-studio potter who ran a pottery in Essex, England, in the 1880s and '90s. Perry consciously eschews even the rough *mingei* finesse of the Leach aesthetic; his potting is indifferent and intentionally

135
KURT WEISER
TEMPE, AZ

Night Harvest, *covered jar, 2002.*
Handbuilt porcelain with china
paint. Purchase 2002 Membership
Endowment Fund, Eleanor S.
Upton Bequest Fund and Franklin
Conklin Memorial Fund
(2002.23.13a, b). Purchased from
the Garth Clark Gallery, New York
City. 17.75"H x 12.5"W x 9"D.

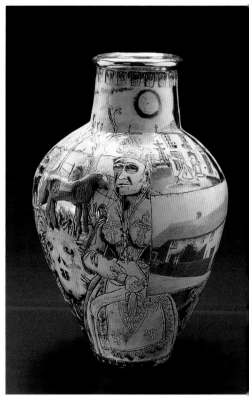

136
GRAYSON PERRY
LONDON, ENGLAND

Essex Man, *1999. Thrown and
altered earthenware with transfer
printed images. Purchase 2002
Membership Endowment Fund,
Mathilde Oestrich Bequest Fund,
Carrie B. F. Fuld Bequest Fund
and Margaret D. Batt Bequest
Fund (2002.23.8). Purchased from
the Garth Clark Gallery, New York
City. 13"H x 9"Dia.*

153

137
ANNE KRAUS
SHORT HILLS, NJ

Irrevocable Steps *tea set, 1986.*
Slipcast white earthenware with
applied glazes. Purchase 1986 The
Members' Fund (86.33a–g).
Purchased from an exhibition at
The Newark Museum. Teapot: 7"H
x 9.5"W x 4.5"D.

heavy. In this case it takes the comforting form of a Chinese jar, and in the decoration of that jar, Perry's work becomes most fascinating. Playing on the English commercial tradition of transfer-printed tablewares, Perry has placed two printed images of mild, manicured suburban cottages on his jar. To that he has added incised and painted images conjuring up a variety of dark, perverse behaviors that might or might not be happening behind the net curtains of the placid small-town exteriors. Like Lucero, Perry uses the pot to make a statement that is compelling in a way that no mere flat painting would ever be.

Anne Kraus, in a work from 1986 entitled *Irrevocable Steps* (fig. 137), offers a decidedly less disturbing narrative. Here the genteel tea set is transformed into a sort of cartoon strip to be read on all sides, including the interior of each piece. Together the four-piece set tells the story of an act that, once done, cannot be undone. Kraus evokes the decorative tea wares that dominated the Euro-American tea ceremony in the last quarter of the 1800s. The square shapes and pagoda-like upturns at the corners suggest the West's fascination with Japanese ceramic and metal forms. By invoking the aesthetic movement in America, Kraus refers to a time when decorative objects were viewed as serious art, the period, in fact, that was the ultimate progenitor of the studio pottery movement.[37] Thus Kraus creates a historical foundation on which she builds the personal (and global) meanings of her narrative.[38]

Mara Superior and Red Weldon Sandlin each make a similar sort of transformation in their fantastical teapots. Superior's work, *A Tea House,* has a sweet, mystical quality (fig. 138). Again using the domestic icon of the teapot, she turns the pot into a house. There is an obvious historic precedent here, in the house-shaped stoneware teapots of eighteenth-century Staffordshire, England. Superior's tea house, however, is monumental and heavy, and sits pretentiously on a gilded wood pedestal. Thus the practical teapot-house of the past has become unwieldy—a massive monument to itself, an unusable, nostalgic reminder of the way we obsess about the "good old days." We are given a further clue to this meaning by the legend "A DREAM" lettered on the front lawn, which is linked to the attached "HOUSE" plaque on the gilded base. From the heart-shaped puffs of smoke issuing from the chimneys (which serve as knobs for the lids) to the roses climbing up the back and the bunnies frolicking on the lawn, the entire piece is a sly, affectionate poke at our longing for a past that never existed.

138
MARA SUPERIOR
WILLIAMSBURG, MA

A Tea House, *1999. Handbuilt and painted porcelain on wooden base. Purchase 2002 Friends of Decorative Arts Fund 2002.9.1a-d). Purchased from the Leslie Ferrin Gallery, Croton-on-Hudson, NY. 16.5"H x 19"W x 8"D.*

This same mixture of affection and irony pervades Red Weldon Sandlin's *Behind Quiet Veils of the Blue Willow* (fig. 139). At its apex sits a pagoda-shaped teapot, evoking Yixing forms as well as the house-shaped teapots of Georgian Staffordshire. The teapot sits on a large tea jar, which is both painted and sculpted in bas-relief. The jar's upper section revolves on concealed ball bearings, and its lower section depicts the eyes, nose and ears of a Chinese man, which appears to be emerging from the water-blue cover of a trompe l'oeil painted book. The color scheme and title evoke the single most popular china pattern ever to hit America. *Blue Willow* was a late-eighteenth-century marketing tool of Josiah Spode, who developed a completely false legend about young Chinese lovers of different social classes who run away from home, are cursed by the girl's father, and thence transformed into doves. Spode originally called the design *Mandarin*,[39] but the presence in the design of what, to Western eyes, appeared to be a weeping willow tree eventually caused it to be renamed *Blue*

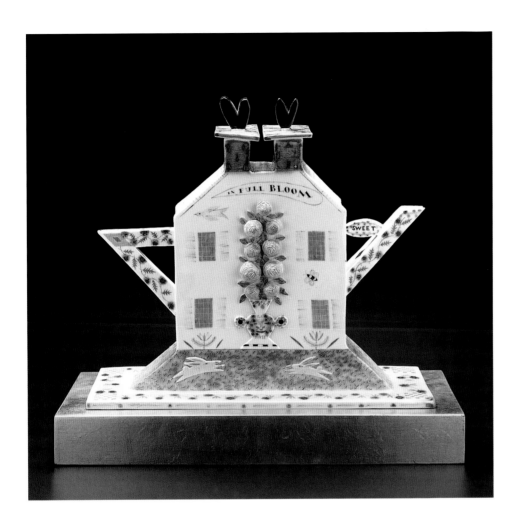

Willow. Sandlin's deconstruction of the *Blue Willow* myth is a commentary on how American popular culture willfully stereotypes, misinterprets and romanticizes other cultures. Of course we, as consumers, buy into it literally and figuratively. The fact that Sandlin's work is gentle, lyrical and visually appealing in no way trivializes the underlying message.

A much darker depiction of our historical relationship with China appears on the extraordinary china-painted teapot by Susan Thayer (fig. 140). Like Kraus, Superior and Sandlin, Thayer uses the familiar, friendly form of the teapot as her narrative vehicle. *Opium Wars* recounts an ugly moment in history when Western commercial demands were brought into violent conflict with Chinese culture. Decorated with the traditional feminine technique of china painting, the teapot is presented as a japanned tea canister, the ship-form finial recalling the means by which the vast wealth of China was linked to the West. The spout is a profile portrait of a stereotyped Chinese merchant or bureaucrat.

Two cartouche-shaped reserves on the long sides of the teapot show strikingly different images. On one, Thayer depicts the burning of the foreign warehouses, or hongs, in Canton in 1839—the ultimate violent reaction against England's longtime support of illegal opium. The other side shows the indistinct image of a naked woman, bringing to mind the odalisques of nineteenth-century painting, but also referring to the extensive white slavery and prostitution that resulted from the opium trade. Thayer's teapot is a more sinister object than those of her peers', and it embodies in its form and narrative decoration the long-standing cultural and commercial tensions between China and the West.

139
RED WELDON SANDLIN
OWENSBORO, KY

Behind Quiet Veils of the Blue Willow, 2001. *Whiteware with painted decoration, painted wood. Gift of Susan Thayer Farago, 2001 (2001.74a-f). 26"H x 12.5"W x 10.5"D.*

140
SUSAN THAYER
PORTLAND, OR

Opium Wars, *2001. Handbuilt and
china-painted porcelain. Purchase
2002 Friends of Decorative Arts
Fund (2002.9.4a, b). Purchased
from the Leslie Ferrin Gallery,
Croton-on-Hudson, NY. 3.75"H x
13.75"W x 2.75"D.*

There is a kind of wise pot that seems to embody a prayerful reverence for clay, a kind of spiritual link between the maker and the medium. This can be manifested in a variety of ways, some more obvious and literal than others. Priscilla Nampeyo's pots evoke her great-grandmother Nampeyo's work, but her own spiritual connection to clay is as much a part of the heritage she carries as are the designs and the technique (fig. 141). "I always pray when I do my pots, and I tell my children to do the same thing,"[40] she said in the early 1990s. The making of the vessel and its decoration thus become a ritual imbued with religious power.

Nancy Adams seems to draw her visual metaphors from Indian culture (fig. 142), but the spiritual connection in her *Spirit Corn Vessel* involves a personal reverence for nature and its power to heal. Indian corn, which since the nineteenth century has been used as an emblem of American values,[41] is dominant in this piece; a variety of images pervades Adams's other work and demonstrate a generalized love of nature and its creations.

Adrian Saxe's elegant, ironic work might not initially seem worshipful, yet it is. Saxe's statement is different from the spiritual worship central to Priscilla Nampeyo's pots or the outdoorsy, pop-culture earth worship of Nancy Adams's colorful pieces. With his remarkably crafted and visually loaded vessels, Saxe pays intelligent homage to the cult of porcelain, which dates back to the discovery of porcelain in the West by Johann Boettger, in a Saxon prison. The rough, yet exquisitely modeled, stoneware antelope finial (fig. 143) nods reverentially to the unbridled energy and beauty of nature, and the sawtoothed upper rim of the jar is a nod to the intriguing cogs and gears of industrial America.[42] Nevertheless, the jar itself is a paean to the beauty of Chinese celadon porcelains and their European counterparts during the eighteenth century. For all his ironic bravado, Saxe is worshiping at an altar, secular though it may be. He is reveling in artifice, in the skill of human hands to fashion amazing materials into objects of glamorous and seductive beauty.

Yet other pots appear to be worshipful by virtue of their presence, by what I have always thought of as a totemic quality. While there does seem to be a ritual

141
**PRISCILLA NAMINGHA
NAMPEYO**
HOPI PUEBLO, AZ

*Seed jar with painted decoration,
1979. Coiled earthenware with
applied engobes. Purchase 1979
Franklin Conklin, Jr., Bequest
Fund (79.625). Purchased from the
Mudd-Carr Gallery, Santa Fe,
NM. 2.5"H x 6.5"Dia.*

142
NANCY ADAMS
SAN GERONIMO, CA

Spirit Corn Vessel, *1988–89.
Thrown and modeled earthenware
with low-fire glazes. Purchase 1989
The Members' Fund and partial gift
of the Sheila Nussbaum Gallery
(89.1). Purchased from the Sheila
Nussbaum Gallery, Millburn, NJ.
14"H x 13"W x 8"D.*

143 *(opposite)*
ADRIAN SAXE
LOS ANGELES, CA

*Antelope jar, 1979. Thrown and
carved porcelain, stoneware.
Purchase 1996 Mrs. James C. Brady
Fund, Carrie B.F. Fuld Bequest
Fund, Franklin Conklin Memorial
Fund and Eleanor S. Upton Bequest
Fund (96.76a, b). Purchased from
Garth Clark Gallery, New York
City. 14.5"H x 8.5"Dia.*

quality in their making, these pieces suggest a ceremonial function, as if they could be used for a sacred ritual of some kind.

Beatrice Wood's gold chalice from 1985 (fig. 144) has a particularly strong ceremonial presence. Footed cups have figured in religious ritual for millennia, and Wood's rough technique, combined with her mysterious many-handled form and the sheen of her gold luster, give this chalice an ancient quality that evokes some long-lost goddess. Robert Turner's work has a totemic aspect, and his use of African words in titles, as in *Dark Ife* and *Ashanti*, shown here (figs. 145, 146), reinforces that aura of solemnity. The verdigris-tinged black glaze used on both of these pieces suggests ancient bronze, as well as both the metalwork and the ceramics of the Akan and Benin cultures.

By enlarging the teapot and wrapping it in a bubbled bronze-green glaze, Anne Hirondelle gives it the power of an archaic Chinese ritual ewer (fig. 147). It is easier to imagine kneeling before it than pouring tea out of it. Much the same spell is cast by Walter Keeler, known for his salt-glazed vessels that are at once traditional and disconnected in time (fig. 148). Derived from a humble milk canister, this lidded jar takes on the elegant dignity of the best rural English utility wares of the eighteenth century, and also the ancient presence of an

144 (*opposite*)
BEATRICE WOOD
OJAI, CA

Chalice with gold luster, 1985. Thrown earthenware. Purchase 1986 Louis Bamberger Bequest Fund (86.4). Purchased from the Garth Clark Gallery, New York City. 12.9"H x 7.6"Dia.

145
ROBERT TURNER
ALFRED, NY

Dark Ife, 1988. Handbuilt and thrown stoneware. Gift of Julia G. and John S. Dietz, 1988 (88.89a, b). 10.75"H x 8"Dia.

146
ROBERT TURNER
ALFRED, NY

Ashanti, 1986. Thrown and handbuilt stoneware. Collection of Sandra and Louis Grotta. 14"H x 11.5"Dia.

147
ANNE HIRONDELLE
PORT TOWNSEND, WA

Luna's Teapot, *1992. Thrown and handbuilt stoneware with bubbled glaze. Purchase 1992 Harry E. Sautter Bequest Fund (92.303a–c). Purchased from the Garth Clark Gallery, New York City. 15"H x 12"W x 8.25"D.*

148
WALTER KEELER
BRISTOL, ENGLAND

Milk-can form jar, late 1980s. Thrown stoneware with salt glaze. Gift of Garth Clark and Mark Del Vecchio (99.72a, b). 12.75"H x 7.75"W x 5.25"D.

149
KAREN KARNES
MORGAN, VT

Vase with cobalt blue salt glaze, ca. 1980. Thrown stoneware. Gift of Alice and Malcolm Nanes, 2001 (2001.57.3). 14.4"H x 10"Dia.

Egyptian canopic vessel. In a like way Karen Karnes, with the subtly asymmetrical outline of her cone-necked salt-glazed vase (fig. 149), gives a simple flower holder a sculptural potency that suggests it should be set on an altar in a temple rather than in a domestic setting.

One aspect of the worshipful vessel is the artist's ritual in making it. Brother Thomas, perhaps because he is a monk, seems instinctively to bring a sense of worship to the throwing of his pristine, Chinese-inspired porcelain vessels (fig. 150). Magdalene Odundo's graceful coiled vessels are captivating; after watching her make one of her pots, one is convinced of the magic in her skill (fig.151). Influenced by the figural vessels of nineteenth-century Mangbetu people, in Africa, Odundo brings many traditions to her work, from ancient Greek slip-decorated vessels to coiled and burnished Southwestern Indian wares. She builds her large pots with a rhythmic grace that induces a sense of awe from anyone lucky enough to witness it. This rhythmic, repetitive quality is part of the making of a worshipful pot, and indeed every thrown vessel can claim something of that quality.

The traditional African ritual vessel has certainly influenced Lawson Oyekan's broad and delicate *Passage Pot* of 1996 (fig. 152). However, unless one looks closely or runs a hand across the soft green surface, one might not notice the hundreds of tiny pinholes, ritually pricked all over the walls, that render it useless *except* as a spiritual container. The young potter John Pagliaro has brought the pinched vessel to an unimagined level of scale and technical proficiency (fig. 153). Like Oyekan's pinholes, the stippling that covers Pagliaro's pots is a reminder of the constant, repetitive movement of his fingers. He builds up his pots with a sort of meditative ritual, revisiting the most ancient human clayworking technique and producing vessels that are totemic, sculptural and filled with a spiritual gentleness.

The late Rudi Staffel's *Light Gatherers*, so called because of the way they use the inherent translucence of porcelain, always seem evanescent and fragile (fig. 154), as if they were offering vessels meant to hold nothing heavier than prayers. The careful, almost textile-like construction of his pots, as well as their ability to capture light, gives them a worshipful character unique in all American studio pottery.

Dutch porcelain master Babs Haenen treats her porcelain quite differently, crumpling and folding it in a way that reminds one of George Ohr (fig. 155).[43]

**150
BROTHER THOMAS
(THOMAS BEZANSON)**
WESTON PRIORY, VT

Bottle vase, 1975. Thrown porcelain with oxblood glaze. Gift of Ellen and Brann Wry in honor of Samuel C. Miller, 1996 (96.58). 13.15"H x 9"Dia.

151 *(opposite)*
MAGDALENE ODUNDO
LONDON, ENGLAND

Vessel with black surface, 1995.
Coiled earthenware. Purchase 1996
Louis Bamberger Bequest Fund
(96.29). Purchased from Anthony
Slayter-Ralph, Santa Barbara, CA.
21.25"H x 12"Dia.

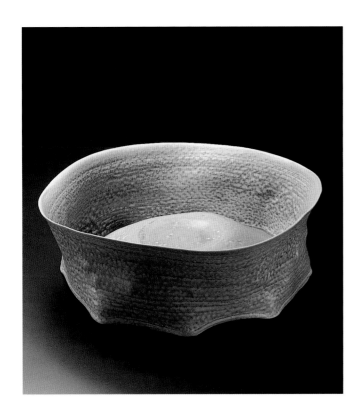

152
LAWSON OYEKAN
LONDON, ENGLAND

Passage Pot, 1996. Thrown and
pierced porcelain with celadon
glaze. Purchase 2002 Membership
Endowment Fund, Estate of
Gertrude Woodcock Simpson,
Henry Puder Bequest Fund and
Franklin Conklin, Jr., Bequest
Fund (2002.23.7). Purchased from
the Garth Clark Gallery, New York
City. 6"H x 19.5"Dia.

153
JOHN PAGLIARO
NEW YORK, NY

Vessel, 2001. Pinched earthenware.
Gift of Garth Clark and Mark Del
Vecchio, 2002 (2002.17). 7.75"H x
11.5"W x 10.5"D.

Here Haenen's ritualized technique is used to evoke another sort of chalice, the spiky-stemmed *roemer* (communal drinking goblet) of seventeenth-century Holland. Prickly and silken at the same time, this vessel, with its rich, fabric-like folds, invokes both the blue-and-white Delft ceramics and the richly striated and fringed tulips that played such pivotal roles in the culture of the seventeenth-century Dutch republic.

Deborah Freed's simple round platter from 1991 (fig. 156) employs a neutral shape in order to capitalize on the luxuriant pattern and color of the painstaking *nerikomi* technique. This technique has its roots in Tang China but was revived in Japan by Kanjiro Kawai in the 1930s.[44] The English also produced tablewares (called "agate ware") in the eighteenth century using a variation on this process. With a very different result from the ritual folding of Staffel or Haenen, *nerikomi* uses colored clays that are folded together repeatedly, then cut and folded again. Precision is needed to control the patterning and distribution of color. *Nerikomi*, like pinching and coiling, requires a meditative yet alert state of mind; the repetitive folding and cutting then become like a ritual incantation.

All of the preceding worshipful pots evoke the presence of the hand of the maker. If some potters, like Elsa Rady, Bill Daley, and Magdalene Odundo,

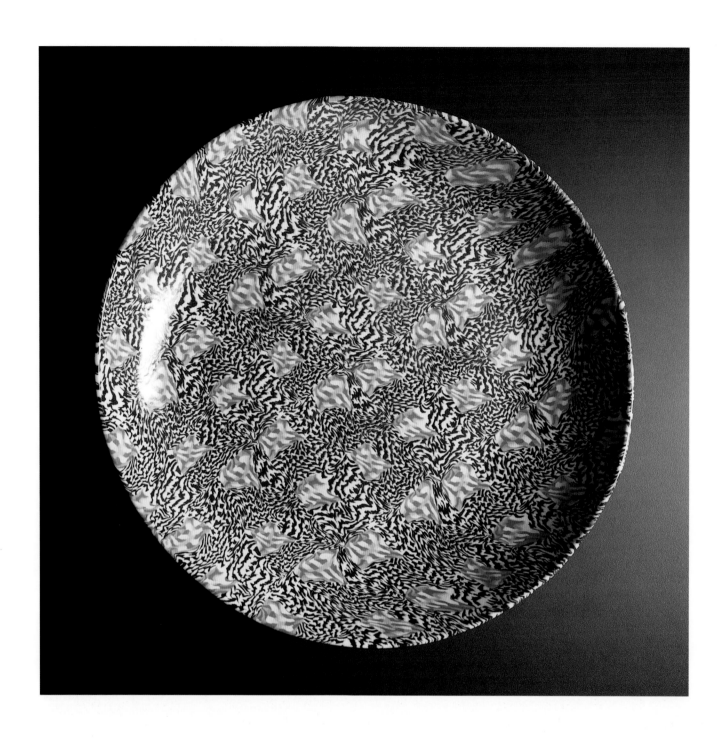

156
DEBORAH FREED
SOMERVILLE, MA

Nerikomi *platter, 1991. Wedged
and formed colored porcelain.
Purchase 1992 Alice W. Kendall
Bequest Fund (92.3). Purchased
from the artist. 1.75"H x 15"Dia.*

174

minimize the evidence of their hand, others, as we have seen, make the physical presence of the potter paramount.

Three very different large plate forms offer a surprisingly parallel sense of the potter's hand, and underscore the fundamental physical power of clay in artistic expression. Unlike the painterly plates, where the format becomes essentially a neutral background for the decoration, with these pieces the form is integral to the perception and meaning of the work. Warren MacKenzie, the American heir to the Leach-Hamada aesthetic, makes his presence known by drawing his fingers through the glaze of a large shallow white bowl from 1979 (fig. 157). This simple human gesture can represent mountains, clouds—or nothing at all. The hands of the potter have destroyed the perfection of the glaze, and at the same time created something new. There is a prayerful serenity to this piece that, in spite of its utilitarian roots, sets it apart as a contemplative object.

Voulkos's big, rough gestural plate from 1981 (fig. 158) is, on the surface, the polar opposite of MacKenzie's. Scratched and prodded, with chunks of porcelain jammed into its face, this plate embodies the kind of virile abstract expressionism that Voulkos used consistently. He saw these plates as three-dimensional drawings—and yet, they are still all about the clay. It is a work of art, regardless of what you call it, that could be made *only* in clay. It's about the broken edges, the cracks and the colors that only clay can give.[45] At the same time, that moment in the early 1950s when a young Peter Voulkos was captivated as he watched Shoji Hamada throw a pot is still present in this plate.[46] Even as Voulkos carried on his career-long rejection of the "perfect pot" and the Japanese aesthetic, he continued to pay homage to the *mingei* tradition.

Neil Tetkowski is from another generation, and his work reflects both his academic training at Alfred and his lifelong interest in world cultures and global issues. The *Dental Mandala* of 1997 (fig. 159) continues the centuries-old tradition of the large charger or bowl as a contemplative artwork. Tetkowski embeds found objects in his huge plates, creating sacred circles, or *mandalas*, a motif common in Buddhist art and symbolizing the unity of creation. This particular work is more personal than global; it was commissioned by the artist's Manhattan dentist. The extracting tools, as well as the impressions around the rim of all the other ritual paraphernalia of the dental office, create a solemn prayer wheel, perhaps reflecting the unspoken prayers of patients in the dentist's outer office as they await treatment.

157 *(opposite)*
WARREN MACKENZIE
STILLWATER, MN

*Large bowl with finger marks,
1979. Thrown and glazed
stoneware. Gift of Garth Clark and
Mark Del Vecchio, 2001
(2001.78.8). 5"H x 20.6"Dia.*

158
PETER VOULKOS
LOS ANGELES, CA

*Plate, 1981. Thrown and altered
stoneware. Purchase 2002
Membership Endowment Fund,
Mrs. James C. Brady Bequest
Fund, Charles W. Engelhard
Bequest Fund and Dr. and Mrs.
Earl LeRoy Wood Fund
(2002.23.4). Purchased from the
Garth Clark Gallery, New York
City. 5"H x 22"Dia.*

159
NEIL TETKOWSKI
NEW YORK, NY

*Dental Mandala, 1997. Handbuilt
earthenware with terra sigilata and
steel elements. Gift of Alice and
Malcolm Nanes, 2001 (2001.57.1).
3"H x 26.5"Dia.*

An important, and even drastic, sea change was wrought on the studio pottery movement by the wise pot during the second half of the 1950s and the early 1960s. The movement was born in Montana and flourished in Los Angeles, and the pots it spawned sent shock waves through the entire studio pottery movement. These pots forever changed the way the vessel would be seen. Much has been written about this movement, and it is, overall, not the focus of this book. Some important examples, however, will shed light on the divergent path that these wise pots took.

John Mason's small-scale but powerful *X Pot* of 1957 is as subversive and radical as any pot of that period (fig. 160). While still, technically, a pot, it moved beyond any reckoning of what a pot was supposed to be in the late fifties and is more a three-dimensional abstract painting or a sculpture. From today's perspective, it is hard to understand just how impossible to comprehend this pot was for the pottery community of the time.

Also "still a pot" is Rudy Autio's large-scale, painterly and sculptural vessel from 1963 (fig. 161). His own growing interest in abstract expressionism, as well as the powerful presence of his colleague Peter Voulkos, led Autio to make a series of big, bulging pots intended to express the artistic impulses of their maker. Eventually the incipient anthropomorphism of these early pots would lead Autio to truly figural work.[47] When one realizes that both Leach and Hamada were still producing and still being celebrated when this big, tough pot was made, one can easily see how such work made heads spin. The effect of this West Coast phenomenon was immediate.

When California-trained Jolyon Hofsted arrived in New York to teach in 1963, he had been influenced by both abstract expressionism and the impossible pottery of Peter Voulkos.[48] He began to make large thrown, altered and painted vessels that showed directly the influence of potters like Voulkos, Autio and Mason. Hofsted's *Form #1 from '65* (fig. 162) was shown at The Newark Museum in 1967 and became the first impossible pot in the museum's collection. One has to keep in mind that, with a few exceptions, East Coast decorative arts curators were not attuned to current trends in ceramics. This

160
JOHN MASON
LOS ANGELES, CA

X Pot, *1957. Handbuilt stoneware with paint. Collection of Linda and Donald Schlenger. 14"H x 9"W x 7.5"D.*

big, gestural, messy pot must have seemed exhilaratingly radical when it was acquired.

Hofsted's inspiration, Peter Voulkos, continued to produce extraordinary pots throughout his career, and continued to explore the nature of clay and volume in new ways. His monumental *Big Jupiter*, from 1994 (fig. 163), embodies all the qualities of his stacked vessels. It is massive, virile, brutal. It seems a world away from Shoji Hamada's little painted bowl of 1950 (fig. 26) and yet the reverence for the material and the tradition of the great pot is ever present.

There are many ways, of course, to be impossible. Once the expressionist ceramics of Jolyon Hofsted and Peter Voulkos became part of the canon, they, too, inevitably gave rise to rebels.

Howard Kottler and Marek Cecula are two inventively subversive ceramic artists whose work has caused as much trauma in the pottery world as Voulkos's and Mason's once did. Kottler's *Grant Wood Ware Set* of 1972 (fig. 164) might best be described as an anti-pot work, with its pop sense of ridiculing its own

source of inspiration. While Adrian Saxe plays with eighteenth-century porcelain traditions, Kottler thumbs his nose at the pretensions of the art museum *and* the preciousness of the studio potter. He rejects the fetishization of handcraft, and lampoons the knee-jerk reverence for so-called fine art. He subverts both Bernard Leach and Peter Voulkos by applying decals of a famous painting to mass-produced dishes. The synthetic damask lining and faux-woodgrain leatherette of the storage envelopes for the dishes create an aura of bogus luxury, while the shrine-like oak box mimics the presentation boxes used by Japanese studio potters. Kottler adopts a sort of Dada sensibility that declares art to be what he says it is, and appropriates pop culture imagery just as Andy Warhol and Roy Lichtenstein did during the same period.[49]

Marek Cecula takes the tradition of appropriation and brings it into a postmodern context. In *Mutant III* (fig. 165) he has picked up on the cozy teapot formula favored by narrative potters, and specifically on the mass-produced neo-rococo porcelain tea wares of central Europe. He transforms these symbols of middle-class continental gentility into witty, creepy commentaries on industrialization and global toxicity. The lids are fused into place, and the set itself is

intentionally incomplete. The tumor-like growths that disfigure the pristine whiteness of the porcelain make these familiar objects alien and frightening, reminders of the man-made causes that increasingly underlie mortality today.

Art Nelson, also trained in California at the height of the funk era, opts for an ironically Leach-like "perfect pot" approach to the impossible pot. His *Black Meta Vessel* of 1984 (fig. 166) is a masterpiece of technique; his vessels are double-walled and thrown with consummate skill and precision. Nelson adopts weird scale and oddball pop colors (here a sort of dusty rose and chartreuse yellow), and then stacks his components, turning them into elegant minimalist sculptures. These works have none of the 1950s-type, earthy, hands-on quality of either MacKenzie's traditionalism (fig. 157) or Voulkos's gestural artistry (fig. 158).

Piet Stockmans, a leading figure in Belgian studio ceramics, uses stacked pots in a gentle update on Kottler's work of the early 1970s. In Stockmans's 1998 *Object with Box* (see fig. 2, page 6), eleven slipcast porcelain dishes of graduated size are dipped in blue glaze and then nested. The artist is commenting on the commercialization and mass production of art and of ceramics,

165
MAREK CECULA
NEW YORK, NY

Mutant III *teapot and sugar bowl, 1998. Porcelain, altered. Purchase 2002 Wallace Scudder Bequest Fund and Membership Endowment Fund (2002.23.3.1,.2). Purchased from the Garth Clark Gallery, New York City Teapot: 6.5"H; sugar bowl: 4"Dia.*

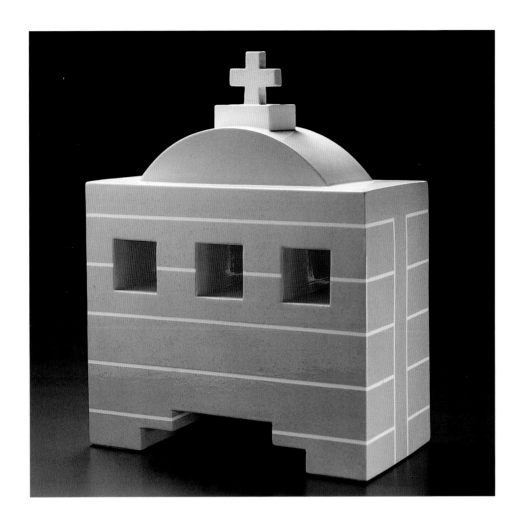

167
MICHAEL DUVALL
BEAR LAKE, MI

Mission Box *(with two lids)*, *1986.*
Slipcast white earthenware with
applied glazes. Purchase 1987
Wallace M. Scudder Bequest Fund
(87.9a-c). Purchased from the
Garth Clark Gallery, New York
City. 15"H x 11.5"W x 6"D.

while also invoking the centuries-old Euro-American fetish for blue-and-white porcelain. Stockmans, who also designs for industrial production, uses the simple pine packing crate as a metaphor parallel to Kottler's shrine box. However, the joke here is less barbed than Kottler's, and the elegant austerity of Stockmans's work, as well as the freedom of the viewer to rearrange it in a way that is most visually pleasing, suggests a traditional Japanese sense of aesthetic pleasure.

Another approach to the impossible pot is the rejection of the functional vessel while retaining a passionate interest in the importance of form and volume. Michael Duvall offers a postmodern homage to architect Michael Graves with his *Mission Box* of 1986 (fig. 167). This piece documents the renewed interest in classical forms, as well as the ornamental approach to architecture on the part of architects such as Graves and Robert A.M. Stern. Duvall positions this postmodern reference in the context of traditional Southwestern architecture with its dominant geometric presence. In Duvall's work, the actual open

166 *(opposite)*
ARTHUR NELSON
OAKLAND, CA

Black Meta Vessel, *1984. Thrown*
stoneware. Gift of Garth Clark and
Mark Del Vecchio, 1986 (86.40a-c).
11.25"H x 20.15"Dia (overall).

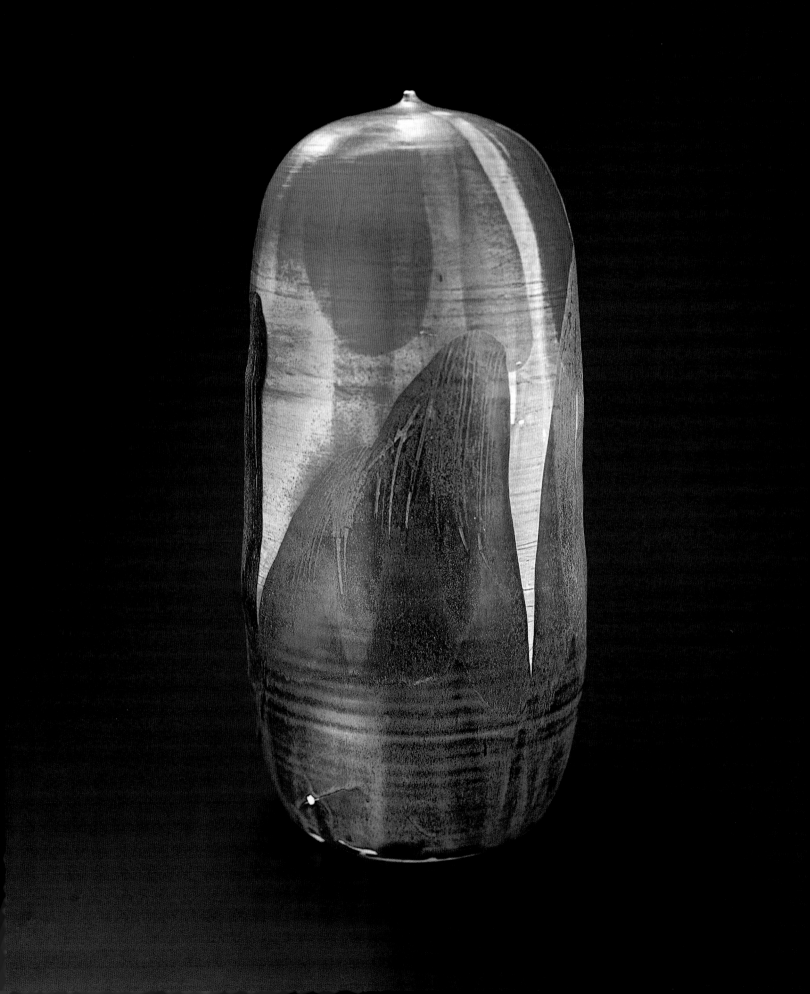

vessel has been minimized to the small curved section on top of the structure, but its strong totemic aspect makes it clear that this is a container for historical memories.

Toshiko Takaezu's closed vessel of about 1990 (fig. 168) is a completely different interpretation of this same idea. Takaezu was from the first generation of ceramic artists to reject the functional vessel without rejecting the pot. For her the volume inside the pot remains a critical aspect of her sculptural forms, and the traditional physical presence of the artist is evident in the throwing of the clay. From this perspective, her closed sculpture forms are still containers, just as mysterious and worshipful today as they were in the late 1960s when she first experimented with closed forms.

German potter Michael Cleff's untitled 1998 work (fig. 169) seems to fall somewhere between Duvall and Takaezu in its approach to the closed pot. His sly shino-glazed form appears to be a pure sculpture, but by connecting the dots—the small openings connected by a thin blue line—one realizes that, as in any traditional vessel, there is an interior volume (the top dot) and a footed

168 *(opposite)*
TOSHIKO TAKAEZU
CINTON, NJ

Closed vessel with pink and purple glazes, ca. 1990. Thrown stoneware. Collection of Irene and Barry Fisher. 19.5"H x 8"Dia.

169
MICHAEL CLEFF
HATTINGEN, GERMANY

Untitled #1. *Vessel with shino glaze, 1998. Handbuilt stoneware. Gift of Garth Clark and Mark Del Vecchio, 2001 (2001.78.5). 14.5"H x 15"W x 11"D.*

base (the lower dot). Thus, while emphatically *not* functional, Cleff's work remains a pot and pays homage to the ceramic traditions of the past.

Robert Arneson was always known as a ceramic sculptor, and he rarely made "pots" in such a direct way as with his *Huddle* of 1973 (fig. 170). Arneson's sculptural brilliance is multiplied in the series of diminutive phallic self-portrait heads that encircle the rim of the of vessel. The "huddle" of the title refers to Arneson's love of football, but there is a darker underlying meaning. Here are seven little selves huddled together discussing something very serious. The bathtub plug attached to the ear of the large head vessel gives a clue: the artist's own oncoming hearing loss. These portraits represent the artist confronting the reality of middle age and the onset of gradual physical decay. The form of the pot, bringing to mind a crown rib roast, is obviously nonfunctional, but the surprise inside the pot—a generously scaled penis that winks up at you from the bottom—is part of a long Western tradition of humorous pottery. Standard items in nineteenth-century utility vessels were pitchers and mugs with ceramic frogs at the bottom, and chamber pots were often made with printed or painted eyes on the inside, or with portraits of political figures. Even in the studio pottery world, the irrepressible George Ohr placed facsimile turds in the bottom of his vessels. Thus Arneson updates a time-honored tradition and brings to it the rebellious, sexually charged atmosphere of his own artistic times. The joke is tempered, however, by the poignant truth behind it, the very real anxiety every man feels about his own virility as he leaves youth and all its physical self-confidence behind.

The three impossible pots shown here by Phillip Maberry, Henry Pim and Cindy Kolodziejski call up the splendid and splashy "palace wares" of the eighteenth and nineteenth centuries, particularly presentation pieces and ceremonial

171
PHILLIP MABERRY
HIGHLAND, NY

Urn on plinth, 1990. Thrown white stoneware with applied glazes. Purchase 1990 The Members' Fund (90.241a, b). Purchased from the Garth Clark Gallery, New York City. 16"H x 21"W x 11.75"D.

189

urns. They all present a postmodern counterpoint to Arneson's bad-boy funk vessel of the 1970s. Large, brightly colored porcelain urns and vases with ormolu mounts were standard features in affluent houses in the decades around 1900. Professional as well as amateur china painters, both men and women, acquired elaborate porcelain blanks and lavished naturalistic floral and figural decoration on them to serve as ornaments in these same lush parlors.[50] At the same time, antique Chinese porcelains and other ancient and "curious" metal and ceramic vessels were collected from all over the world, giving Euro-American home owners a comfortable sense that the world was within their grasp.

Each of these artists' work evokes some aspect of that past ceramic culture, and then spins it in a late-twentieth-century way. Maberry, rather than looking at literature or nature as the china painters did, looks to television and advertising

172
HENRY PIM
LONDON, ENGLAND

Footed two-handled vessel, 1985. Handbuilt stoneware. Gift of Garth Clark and Mark Del Vecchio, 2001 (2001.78.7). 8.5"H x 14.5"W x 12"D.

173
CINDY KOLODZIEJSKI
VENICE, CA

Clapping Monkey/Banana *ewer,*
2000. Slipcast whiteware with
painted decoration. Purchase 2002
Sophronia Anderson Bequest Fund
(2002.23.12). Purchased from the
Garth Clark Gallery, New York
City. 11.5"H x 8"W x 4.75"D.

174
RON NAGLE
SAN FRANCISCO, CA

Vermilion to One, *2000.*
Whiteware with enamel glazes.
Purchase 2002 Membership
Endowment Fund, Emma Fantone
Endowment (2002.23.5).
Purchased from the Garth Clark
Gallery, New York City. 6.75"H x
5.75"W x 4.6"D.

175
KEN PRICE
LOS ANGELES, CA

Geometric cup, 1980. Slipcast
porcelain. Collection of Linda and
Donald Schlenger. 6.75"H x 5.75"W.

192

for his decorative inspiration (fig. 171). Pop culture, not high culture, inspires his flashy colors and linear graphic style. The polka dots painted on the interior suggest the packaging of Wonder Bread, and the gold-luster ribbon handles refer both to nineteenth-century ormolu handles and to Roy Lichtenstein's brushstroke paintings of the late 1960s.

Henry Pim is not interested in content as much as in breaking with the traditional pottery mystique in his native England. His pots conjure up ancient Chinese vessels, their carved verdigris surfaces rough with muted color and pattern (fig. 172). Pim employs cardboard forms to build his vessels even when his shapes could readily be thrown; in doing so, he rejects the Leach-Hamada concept of making a pot.

Kolodziejski's china-painting skills are superb, and she renders familiar objects—a wind-up childhood toy (fig. 173) and a perfectly ordinary piece of fruit—in a way that is at once realistic and repellent. It's as if one hadn't truly looked at these things before, and from the artist's viewpoint they become vaguely threatening. Just as Victorian and Edwardian china painters covered their porcelain canvases with banalities, so does Kolodziejski, but with a twist that sends a shiver down the viewer's spine.

Both Ron Nagle and Ken Price have been making impossible pots of a very different order from those of their peers since the early 1960s. Both artists have totally rejected the canon of clay work that began the studio pottery movement, and the objects they make (figs.174, 175) are obviously more art than pottery. These works have a stunning artificiality that sets them apart; their bright colors, slick surfaces and coolly calculated, nongestural forms all make them cerebral, inhuman and enigmatic. Yet they are both pots, impossible or not. They both have openings, and their sculptural power is dependent upon the volumes they enclose—the viewer is aware of the interior space as an essential part of the identity of these pots. They are still containers for ideas, and in that they remain true to their tradition.

Leopold Foulem, a Canadian artist, takes this kind of impossible pot to its logical extreme with his brilliant red abstraction from 1999 (fig. 176). It is cast in a one-piece mold, and remains open at the bottom. This work is purely nonfunctional; it is a sculpture of the *idea* of a chocolate pot on a stand. Foulem's work discards the human interaction of creation in much the same way Andy Warhol's "factory-made" paintings confounded notions of artistic production

in the 1960s. Foulem's red pot is all about form and color. Its pristine, precise geometric forms are part of the postmodern revival of classicism. Yet it, too, is still a pot. It pays homage to every beautiful, classic vessel ever made; it evokes all the same emotions that a cozy domestic artifact might stir up. By its vehement inutility it claims its right—and in some ways claims the right for all decorative arts objects—to be looked at as seriously as the sculptures of Auguste Rodin or Constantin Brancusi or Claes Oldenburg, as seriously as any work of art. It provokes a visceral reaction of pleasure; then it provokes puzzlement, irritation, laughter and, ultimately, thought. In the end, it is a very wise pot.

IN CONCLUSION

As a final comment, I'd like to compare a very difficult pot with a very easy pot. Consider once again the first pot in this essay, Ruth Kenly's elegant little bowl from 1959 (see page 24, fig. 8). Compare it with Andrew Lord's large, bombastic, sculptural, impossible pot from 1992 titled *Vase. Pressing and Squeezing* (fig. 177). How can these works be in the same universe, much less appeal to the same curator?

These two potters, the unknown suburbanite from New Jersey and the much-reviewed English-born sculptor from Manhattan, in spite of all the differences in their work and their very different perspectives, are telling the same story. Lord has an intense personal interaction with his vessels. With this one, from a series made in 1992 and displayed together as a group,[51] he pressed and squeezed the clay between his hands "with as much force as possible" as he built it up into a complex, tortured form that he calls, simply, a "vase." The lumpy, visceral surface that comes out of his technique holds the memory of his actions, the history of his physical contact with the clay.[52]

Thus, while Lord's intellectual response to his work is presumably more complex than was Kenly's, it is nonetheless, like hers, a highly personal connection

176
LEOPOLD FOULEM
MONTREAL, QUEBEC, CANADA

Abstraction 5211 (Red), *1999. Slipcast whiteware with red glaze. Purchase 2002 Louis Bamberger Bequest Fund, Sophronia Anderson Bequest Fund and Membership Endowment Fund (2002.23.2). Purchased from the Garth Clark Gallery, New York City. 7"H x 7.5"W x 6.6"D.*

with the material—that same human response to clay that provoked and inspired Bernard Leach, Shoji Hamada, Henry Varnum Poor and Peter Voulkos. Also like Kenly's bowl, Lord's vase is highly concerned with the glaze; the subtle and lustrous surface of Lord's pot is as delicate and sensual as the shimmering taffeta of a Worth evening gown. Furthermore, Lord spatters his vase with gilded epoxy that gives the effect of molten gold, and this same gold covers the tiny, vestigial legs that give the vase stability. Here the hip modern artist is making a scholarly reference to Japanese ceramic restoration techniques—a reference that few in the modern fine-art world would appreciate but that ceramic scholars would understand immediately. Aesthetically, Lord's work offers a very different experience than does Kenly's smooth surface and calligraphic squiggles, but it shows an equally intense concern for the surface of the pot.

Perhaps, after all, Ruth Kenly and Andrew Lord aren't so far apart. Both artists use their medium with skill, patience, intelligence and wisdom. Both created pots that are, as a result, beautiful, contemplative and wise. If there is a real distinction, it is in their understanding of what a pot can be. For Kenly, a pot was a pot, and a pot knew its place. For Lord, a pot knows its place as well—but that place is no longer on a coffee table or a sideboard.

In the final analysis, what has changed most since the studio pottery movement began is not the nature of pottery, but the perception of art. Art at the beginning of the twenty-first century is completely different from what it was in 1900, and what defines fine art is no longer what used to define it. A great pot, on the other hand, is still a great pot, and for the same reasons: the clay, the surface, the shape, the color and the artist's relationship with all of these elements. Some things never change.

NOTES

PREFACE

1. This has been done and done well. For example, see Jo Lauria, *Color and Fire: Defining Moments in Studio Ceramics, 1950–2000*, Los Angeles and New York: Los Angeles County Museum of Art and Rizzoli, 2000; Barbara Perry (ed.), *American Ceramics: The Collection of Everson Museum of Art*, Syracuse and New York: Everson Museum of Art and Rizzoli, 1989; Garth Clark, *American Ceramics, 1876 to the Present*, New York: Abbeville Press, 1987.

ESSAY

1. See Michael K. Komanecky, *American Potters: Edwin and Mary Scheier*, Manchester, NH: The Currier Gallery of Art, 1993, p. 58.
2. The Newark Museum displayed this beverage set on a modern coffee table in a living room vignette. See "Modern Design at The Newark Museum, A Survey" by Dean Freiday, in *The Museum*, vol. IV, nos. 1 and 2, Winter–Spring, 1952, p. 16.
3. Komanecky, *American Potters*, p. 45. The Newark Museum acquired a piece by Binns in 1926.
4. Martha Drexler Lynn, "Adrian Saxe and the Cultured Pot," in *The Clay Art of Adrian Saxe*, Los Angeles and London: Los Angeles County Museum of Art and Thames & Hudson, 1993, p. 46, fig 12.
5. See my article, "Paul St. Gaudens and the Emerging Studio Pottery Movement," in Henry Duffy (ed.) *Paul St. Gaudens, Ceramic Artist*, Cornish, NH: Saint-Gaudens National Memorial, 2001, pp. 27–35.
6. See Anne Spencer, *Tempered by Time: 800 Years of Southwest Indian Pottery in The Newark Museum*. Newark: The Newark Museum, 1983, p. 29.
7. See Leach's *A Potter's Book*, London: Faber and Faber, 1953 (first published 1939).
8. In particular Robineau's masterpiece, *The Apotheosis of the Toiler*, 1910, popularly called the *Scarab Vase*, in the collection of the Everson Museum of Art in Syracuse, NY.
9. Letter from Marguerite McIntosh, April 2, 2002, Newark Museum object files.
10. Brother Thomas, "Contemplative Values in My Work," in *The Porcelains of Brother Thomas: The Path to the Beautiful*, Boston: David R. Godine and the Pucker Safrai Gallery, 1987, pp. 3–5.
11. For the Nampeyo genealogy see Rick Dillingham, *Fourteen Families in Pueblo Pottery*, Albuquerque: University of New Mexico Press, 1994, pp.14–15.
12. Letter to the author from Beatrice Wood, March 15, 1986. Newark Museum object files.
13. Poor's book, *A Book of Pottery: From Mud into Immortality*, Englewood Cliffs, NJ: Prentice-Hall, 1958, makes no mention of either Shoji Hamada or Bernard Leach. But Leach wrote to Poor and praised the book because of the sympathy he felt for Poor's perspective on clay (Clark, *American Ceramics*, pp. 290–91).
14. Soetsu Yanagi, *The Unknown Craftsman: A Japanese Insight into Beauty*, Tokyo, New York, London: Kodansha International, 1972 (revised edition 1989), p. 16, color plate 6.
15. Baekeland and Robert Moes, *Modern Japanese Ceramics in American Collections*, New York: Japan Society, 1993, p. 121.
16. See Spencer, *Tempered by Time*, p. 30. It is interesting to note that The Newark Museum purchased this piece from Rick Dillingham, a studio potter in his own right, who made his pots by breaking and rebuilding the fragments of his work.
17. Susan Peterson, *Pottery by American Indian Women: The Legacy of Generations*, New York: Abbeville Press, and the National Museum of Women in the Arts, 1997, p. 100.
18. An example is in the Campbell Soup Collection at the H.F. duPont Winterthur Museum, Winterthur, DE.
19. For more on Eberle's work of this format, see Forrest J. Snyder's review, "Ed Eberle: Drawing on a Cultural Engramme," of the exhibition "Drawings on Paper and Porcelain" at the Columbus Museum of Art, January 16–March 21, 1999; website: Critical Ceramics (http://criticalceramics.org/reviews/shows/nc99eber.htm).
20. The Newark Museum owns the sheet of drawings worked up for this piece in 1986, given by Mr. and Mrs. Thomas Daley in 2002. See also, *William Daley, Ceramic Works and Drawings*, Philadelphia: Levy Gallery for the Arts in Philadelphia, Moore College of Art and Design, 1993.

21. Author's correspondence with the artist, March 25, 2002. Newark Museum object files.
22. Her children, Dusty and Forrester Naranjo, are well-known potters today.
23. See Leach's *The Potter's Book*, ff. p. 35, fig. 20.
24. See *American Potters: Mary and Edwin Scheier*, pp. 62–63.
25. Woodman confirmed by telephone that these pieces were indeed meant to be used for serving breads and cakes, April 2002.
26. In particular, a silver tea service called *The Diamond* was designed after this sort of shape by John C. Prip of the Rhode Island School of Design in Providence for Reed and Barton in 1958. An example of this service is in The Newark Museum collection.
27. See Clark, *American Ceramics*, p. 305.
28. See Garth Clark, *The Potter's Art.* London: Phaidon, 1995, p. 168.
29. Interestingly, the Los Angeles County Museum of Art owns an identical teapot by the artist, purchased at the same Copenhagen store, Den Permanente, at the same time as the Newark example. See Martha Drexler Lynn, *Clay Today: Contemporary Ceramists and Their Work*, Los Angeles and San Francisco: Los Angeles County Museum of Art and Chronicle Books, 1990, p. 190.
30. I must note that this color is impossible to photograph. The true color approaches emerald, with a strong hint of a grassy tone.
31. A similar shift in scale took place in European and American teapots from the eighteenth to the nineteenth century, as tea became cheaper and was consumed in ever-larger quantities. As Americans got richer and more aristocratic in their taste, their teapots got larger and more elaborate. Oddly enough, however, with the sudden Western interest in Yixing and Japanese tea wares in the last quarter of the nineteenth century, there was again a diminution of scale in Euro-American teapots, suggesting that there was a coincident awareness of and appreciation for Asian scale in Western teapots.
32. Only one Westerner has ever been allowed to design teapots for production at the Yixing kilns. Gerald Gulotta, of New York City, produced a set of seven Yixing teapots in the 1990s. Examples of these are in the collection of the Cooper-Hewitt National Design Museum, New York, and at The Newark Museum.
33. The Everson Museum, Syracuse, NY, owns one of the clearest examples of these, *Little Egret*, from 1992. See Dorothy Weiss, *Annette Corcoran, Birds and Teapots, 1987–1996*, San Francisco: Dorothy Weiss Gallery, 1996.
34. Komanecky, *American Potters*, p. 52.
35. The French painter Paul Gauguin fashioned a portrait of himself as a jug in 1889. This small piece (7.6"H) is in the Museum of Decorative Art, Copenhagen. It is made of stoneware and glazed in olive green and red.
36. Entirely unrecognized in his own lifetime, Ohr nonetheless produced an immense body of work that surfaced in the early 1970s, making him instantly famous. See Garth Clark, Robert Ellison and Eugene Hecht, *The Mad Potter of Biloxi: The Art and Life of George E. Ohr*, New York: Abbeville Press, 1989.
37. The best overall study of this is Doreen Bolger Burke et al., *In Pursuit of Beauty: Americans and the Aesthetic Movement*, New York: The Metropolitan Museum, 1986.
38. There seem to be very few male china painters in contemporary ceramics today. Matt Nolen, of New York City, is one. He uses narrative vessels in a way similar to that of Anne Kraus. His work, for all its decorative qualities, is dark and often deals with wrenching modern issues such as AIDS and urban violence.
39. In the late 1920s, Spode was still marketing this design as *Mandarin*. The Newark Museum purchased several pieces for its collection at that time.
40. Rick Dillingham, *Fourteen Families in Pueblo Pottery*, Albuquerque: University of New Mexico Press, 1994, p. 65.
41. For a discussion of Indian corn's symbolism, see Mary Warner Blanchard, "Candace Wheeler's Search for the Aesthetic Life," in her book *Oscar Wilde's America: Counterculture in the Gilded Age*, New Haven: Yale University Press, 1998, pp. 45-75.
42. See *The Clay Art of Adrian Saxe*, pp. 22, 31.
43. See note 36.
44. See Baekeland, *Modern Japanese Ceramics in American Collections*, p. 24.
45. See Rose Slivka, "The Artist and His Work: Risk and Revelation," in Rose Slivka and Karen Tsujimoto, *The Art of Peter Voulkos*, Oakland: The Oakland Museum and Kodansha International, p. 36.
46. See Lauria, *Color and Fire*, p. 128.
47. See Clark, *American Ceramics*, p. 253.
48. Correspondence with Hofsted, May 7, 2002. Newark Museum object files.
49. Kottler is also lampooning the notion of "fine china" that is purchased at great expense, then stored away and never used.
50. Edward Lycett was an English-born china painter who, along with his son William, pioneered professional china painting in the United States. The Newark Museum owns examples by both father and son. William H. Morley was another celebrated English-born china painter who worked for Walter Scott Lenox in Trenton, first at his Ceramic Art Company, then at Lenox China. Examples of his work are also in The Newark Museum collection.
51. The showing was at the 65 Thompson Street Gallery in Manhattan, and was titled: "Modelling: A Sculpture of 27 Pieces and Related Works." The various segments of the exhibition were Round, Modelling, Touching & Holding, Marking, Pressing & Squeezing, Fist, and Palm. Newark Museum object files.
52. Letter to the author, May 3, 2002. Newark Museum object files.

ADDITIONAL STUDIO CERAMICS IN THE COLLECTION OF THE NEWARK MUSEUM

Anna Adams
England
Fledgling, 1960. Coiled earthenware, tooled. Purchase 1960 (60.495). Purchased from Heal & Son, Ltd., London. 6"H x 8.25"W x 4.25"D.

Bennett Bean
Blairstown, NJ
Bowl, 1980. Wood-fired earthenware, with applied glazes and paints. Purchase 1980 Thomas L. Raymond Bequest Fund (80.405). Purchased from the artist from a one-person show at The Newark Museum. 6.25"H x 11.25"W x 11"D.

Brother Thomas (Thomas Bezanson)
Weston Priory, VT
Vase, 1991. Thrown porcelain with oxblood glaze. Gift of Mr. and Mrs. Bernard Pucker, Pucker Gallery, Boston, 1991 (91.41). 10.25"H x 9.25"Dia.

Claude Conover
Cleveland, OH
Kaamil, 1985. Thrown stoneware. Gift of the artist and the Sheila Nussbaum Gallery, 1986 (86.219). 22"H x 12"Dia.

Derek Davis
England
Vase, 1966. Thrown stoneware. Purchase 1966 (66.51). Purchased from Primavera Gallery, London. 11.8"H x 3.5"Dia.

Gary DiPasquale
New York, NY
Pair of bowls, 1991. Handbuilt earthenware with applied glazes. Gift of the artist, 1991 (91.79a, b). 3.5"H x 8.15"Dia.

Marcello Fantoni
Florence, Italy
Vase with design of three women, 1950–60. Thrown earthenware with applied slips. Gift of Martin Adler, 1991 (91.25). 16"H x 4.75"Dia.

Arthur Floyd
New York, NY
Covered jar, 1959. Thrown earthenware with glazes. Purchase 1959 (59.355). Purchased from the artist. 11"H x 6"W x 6.25"D.

Henry Gernhardt
Syracuse, New York
Bowl with bright blue matte glaze, 1965. Thrown stoneware. Purchase 1966 (66.608). Purchased from the artist. 5"H x 7.6"Dia.

Alexander Giampietro
Washington, DC
Asymmetrical stoneware dish, 1948. Purchase 1949 (49.367). Purchased from the artist at the Institute of Contemporary Arts, Washington, DC. 3.4"H x 15"W x 10.5"D.

Alexander Giampietro
Washington, DC
Asymmetrical stoneware dish, 1948. Purchase 1949 (49.368). Purchased from the artist at the Institute of Contemporary Arts, Washington, DC. 1.8"H x 11.6"W x 9.25"D.

Kelsea Griffin Gillette
Dover, NH
Shallow bowl with flower holder, 1937–38. Red earthenware with gray-blue and gray-pink satin glaze. Gift of Alice W. Kendall, 1938 (38.587a, b). 1.6"H x 8.25"Dia.

Clyde Gobble
Lexington, NC
Casserole and plate, 1970s. Thrown stoneware. Gift of Vivienne Katz, 1996 (97.67.13a-c). 7.25"H x 10.5"W x 9.25"D.

Clyde Gobble
Lexington, NC
Skillet, 1970s. Thrown stoneware. Gift of Vivienne Katz, 1996 (97.67.14). 4.25"H x 12.9"W x 9.15"D.

Clyde Gobble
Lexington, NC
Juicer, 1970s. Thrown stoneware. Gift of Vivienne Katz, 1996 (97.67.15). 3"H x 8"W x 7.4"D.

Clyde Gobble
Lexington, NC
Dessert set (deep dish and cups), 1970s. Thrown stoneware. Gift of Vivienne Katz, 1996 (97.67.16a-h). Dish: 3.15"H x 12.75"W x 11.6"D; cups: 3"H x 3.25"Dia.

Albert Green
Westfield, NJ
Large bell-shaped footed bowl, 1959. Stoneware with painted decoration. Gift of Hortense Green in memory of Betty Freudenheim, 1997 (97.28). 10.75"H x 13.5"Dia.

Dorothy Hafner
New York, NY
Confetti teapot, 1989. Handbuilt porcelain with applied glazes. Purchase 1989 Estate of Pearl Gross Lee (89.26a, b). Purchased from the artist. 8.5"H x 7.15"W x 3.15"D.

Dorothy Hafner
New York, NY
Fireflies dinner plate and salad bowl, 1989. White earthenware with applied glazes. Purchase 1989 Estate of Pearl Gross Lee (89.27a, b). Purchased from the artist. Dinner plate: 1.25"H x 10.2"W x 10.2"D.

Anthony Hepburn
England
Bowl with mauve splash, 1966. Thrown stoneware. Purchase 1966 (66.54). Purchased from Heal & Son, Ltd., London. 6"H x 9.25"Dia.

Wayne Higby
Alfred, NY
Canyon Krater, 1977. Raku-fired earthenware. Purchase 1988 The Members' Fund (88.101). Purchased from Robert Mehlman, New York City. 7.9"H x 14"W x 9.75"D.

Mary Lou Higgins
Pittsboro, NC
Circuit of Hopes, Circle of Dreams, ca. 1987. Handbuilt white earthenware with applied glazes and lusters. Gift of the artist and the Sheila Nussbaum Gallery, 1988 (88.99). 11.5"H x 13"Dia.

Ka-Kwong Hui
Caldwell, NJ
Sculptural form, 1974. Handbuilt earthenware with polychrome glazes. Gift of Beverly and Herbert Paskow, 1991 (91.78). 16.25"H x 14.25"W x 7.75"D.

Ka-Kwong Hui
Caldwell, NJ
Small Fish Screen, 1987. Handbuilt stoneware. Gift of Mr. and Mrs. Reuben F. Richards, 1988 (88.88). Purchased from the artist, from an exhibition at The Newark Museum. 22"H x 24"W x 7.75"D.

Margaret Israel
New York, NY
Double gourd pierced basket, 1980s. Thrown porcelain with sponged decoration. Gift of Lawrence and Sally Israel, 1989 (89.20). 12.25"H x 7.5"Dia.

Mineo Kato (Okabe)
Nagoya, Japan
Plate, 1955. Thrown earthenware with copper-green glaze. Purchase 1956 (56.329). Purchased in Tokyo. 1.75"H x 12.75"Dia.

Mineo Kato (Okabe)
Nagoya, Japan
Sake bottle and cup, 1954. Thrown earthenware with painted decoration. Purchase 1956 (56.330a, b). Purchased in Tokyo. Bottle: 4.75"H x 3"Dia; cup: 1.9"H x 1.9"Dia.

Richard Kjaergaard
Copenhagen, Denmark
Small pitcher with tooled surface, 1955. Thrown earthenware with gray and rose glazes. Purchase 1956 John B. Morris Fund (56.132). Purchased from Den Permanente, Copenhagen. 6"H x 5.5"W x 4.6"D.

Marion Munk Levinston
Highland Park, NJ
Rectangular vase, 1967. Handbuilt redware. Purchase 1968 Membership Endowment Fund (68.6). Purchased from the artist. 19.5"H x 6"W x 5.75"D.

Daniel Levy
New York, NY
Cup and cake plate, 1988. Handbuilt earthenware. Gift of Samuel C. Miller, 1988 (88.96a, b). 3.9"H x 7.25"W x 8"D.

Stig Lindberg
Gustavsberg, Sweden
Vase, 1959. Thrown stoneware with green glaze. Purchase 1959 (59.25). Purchased from Bonnier's, New York City. 6.5"H x 2.4"Dia.

Michelangelo Marchi
Verona, Italy
Pair of red luster bottle-vases, 1991. Thrown earthenware. Gift of the Vissi d'Arte Gallery, New York City, 1992 (92.37a, b). 14"H x 9"Dia.

Elva Nampeyo
Hopi Pueblo, AZ
Miniature pot with black-and-white decoration, 1960s. Coiled earthenware with applied engobes. Gift of Dr. Edwin R. Littmann, 1967 (67.423). 2.5"H x 3.6"Dia.

Bryan Newman
Somerset, England
Sculptural form, 1966. Handbuilt earthenware. Purchase 1966 (66.55). Purchased from Primavera Gallery, London. 25"H x 2.2"W x 2.4"D.

Bonnie Ntshalintshali
Winston, South Africa
Expulsion, 1997. Handbuilt and modeled terra-cotta with paint. Purchase 1997 Dr. and Mrs. Earl LeRoy Wood Fund (97.73a–e). Purchased from the Ardmore Ceramic Art Studio, Winterton, South Africa. 33.4"H x 11"W x 7.75"D.

Lynn Peters
Plainfield, NJ
Interior Landscape, 1995. Handbuilt earthenware with applied glazes. Gift of the artist, 1996 (96.49). 20.9"H x 17.25"W x 6.25"D.

Lynn Peters
Plainfield, NJ
Teapot, 1997. Thrown and handbuilt redware with tooled surface. Gift of the artist, 1997 (97.35a, b). 7.5"H x 11.15"W x 5.5"D.

Roddy Reed
Tampa, FL
Small rounded vessel, 1990. Pinched earthenware with applied glaze and luster. Gift of the artist, 1991 (91.52). 3.6"H x 5"Dia.

John Reeve
Longlands, England
Cylindrical vase, 1966.
Handbuilt earthenware.
Purchase 1966 (66.53).
Purchased from Primavera
Gallery, London. 8.5"H x
8.75"W x 5.75"D.

Emily Rose
New York, NY
Mountain Chalice, 1972.
Thrown earthenware with
incised decoration. Purchase
1972. Thomas L. Raymond
Bequest Fund (72.163).
Purchased from the artist.
9.4"H x 5.75"Dia.

James Rothrock
Los Angeles, CA
Chalice, 1989. Handbuilt
porcelain. Purchase 1990 O.W.
Casperson Bequest Fund
(90.219). Purchased from the
artist. 10.6"H x 6"W x 6.25"D.

Rodney Rouse
Trenton, NJ
Ming-style vase, 1972. Thrown
porcelain with oxblood
reduction glaze. Purchase 1972
Alice W. Kendall Bequest Fund
(72.174). Purchased from the
artist. 11.6"H x 5"Dia.

Dorothy Delight Rushmore
Madison, NJ
Conical bowl, 1936.
Earthenware with lavender
glaze. Gift of Dorothy Delight
Lewis, 1987 (87.67). 3.25"H x
7"Dia.

Dorothy Delight Rushmore
Madison, NJ
Bell-shaped footed bowl with
design of cats, ca. 1936.
Earthenware with glaze and
painted decoration. Gift of
Dorothy Delight Lewis, 1987
(87.66). 5"H x 4.5"Dia.

Frances Senska
Bozeman, MT
Bough pot with multiple
necks, 1989. Thrown
earthenware, incised. Gift of
Dr. Thomas Folk, 1990
(90.218). 14"H x 7"Dia.

Sy Shames
Basking Ridge, NJ
Slab vase, 1971. Handbuilt
stoneware. Purchase 1971
Thomas L. Raymond Bequest
Fund (71.66). Purchased from
the Annex Gallery, Montclair,
NJ. 12.6"H x 8.25"W x 3.75"D.

Sy Shames
Basking Ridge, NJ
Three sculptural vases, 1977.
Handbuilt porcelain. Purchase
1978 The Members' Fund
(78.457a–c). Purchased from
the artist. 11.5"H x 4.5"W x
4.75"D (largest).

Kit-Yin T. Snyder
Bryn Mawr, PA
White cylindrical vase,
1967–68. Handbuilt porcelain.
Purchase 1968 Membership
Endowment Fund (68.4).
Purchased from the artist.
11.75"H x 5.75"Dia.

Barbara Sorensen
Winter Park, FL
Pandora Wan 91–97, 1997.
Handbuilt stoneware. Gift
of Ronald A. Kuchta, 1998
(98.66a, b). 12.5"H x 7"W
x 6"D.

Toshiko Takaezu
Quakertown, NJ
Closed vessel, 1982 (made at
Newark Museum). Thrown
stoneware with painted
decoration. Gift of the artist,
1983 (83.402). 10.5"H x
10.5"Dia.

David Voll
Hammonton, NJ
Covered vessel, 1985. Thrown
porcelain with celadon glaze.
Purchase 1985 Charles Edison
Bequest Fund (85.328).
Purchased from the artist.
5.5"H x 9.5"W x 9.75"D.

Alan Wallwork
England
Slab vase, 1966. Handbuilt
stoneware. Purchase 1966
(66.424). Purchased from Heal
& Son, Ltd., London. 8.5"H x
10.25"W x 2.75"D.

Carl Walters
Woodstock, NY
Figure of a bull, 1948. White
earthenware, painted
decoration. Purchase 1949
Special Purchase Fund
(49.363). Purchased from
Associated American Artists,
New York City. 10"H x 15"W
x 4.75" D.

Greg Wenz
Shrewsbury, NJ
Vase, 1985. Thrown porcelain
with applied glazes. Purchase
1985 Charles Edison Bequest
Fund (85.326). Purchased
from the Lee Sclar Gallery,
Morristown, NJ. 9"H x
9.25"Dia.

Nancy Wickham
New York, NY
Large plate, 1948. Thrown
stoneware with carved surface.
Purchase 1949 (49.375).
Purchased from the artist.
1.75"H x 12.5"Dia.

Peter K. Wright
Monkton Combe, England
Asymmetrical bowl with three
legs, 1960. Thrown and shaped
stoneware. Purchase 1960
(60.518). Purchased from the
Crafts Centre of Great
Britain, London. 6.25"H x
12.6"W x 10.5"D.

William Wyman
Scituate, MA
Black sculptural vessel, 1977.
Thrown and altered
earthenware. Gift of Marilyn
Pappas, 1991 (91.80). 18.5"H x
8.5"W x 6.5"D.

Robert Zerlin
Freehold, NJ
Owl #7, 1959. Handbuilt
stoneware with speckled
interior glaze. Purchase 1959
(59.75). Purchased from the
artist. 11.75"H x 7.5"W x
6.5"D.

203

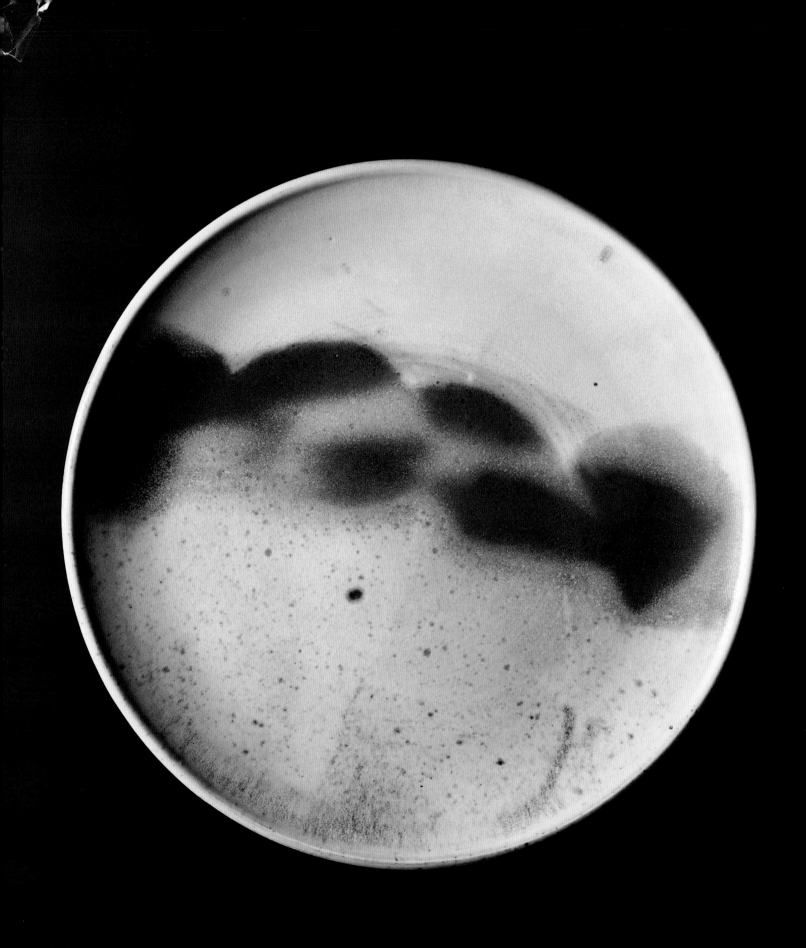

ACKNOWLEDGMENTS

178
TOSHIKO TAKAEZU
CLINTON, NJ

Plate, 1971. Thrown porcelain with painted decoration. Purchase 1971 Thomas L. Raymond Bequest Fund (71.69). Purchased from the artist. 1"H x 11.4"Dia.

This book would not exist if Linda Leonard Schlenger had not made a remarkable offer at the opening of a show at the Garth Clark Gallery in the spring of 2001. As we chatted about the work and about collecting, Linda mentioned that the Friends of Contemporary Ceramics would like to underwrite the cost of a book based on The Newark Museum's collection of contemporary ceramics. It had long been my dream to follow up on the museum's 1984 publication about our art pottery collection. The generosity of the Friends of Contemporary Ceramics at last made this possible.

Althea Meade-Hajduk, who assisted in preparing this volume, has been a joy to have as a colleague. She has encouraged me, inspired me, gently corrected me and steadied my faltering steps. I would also like to thank those generous collectors who allowed us to photograph and include masterworks from their personal collections; these pieces broaden the scope of this book and fill the most glaring gaps in our holdings. In particular I am grateful to (in alphabetical order) Garth Clark and Mark Del Vecchio; Richard DeVore; Irene and Barry Fisher; Sandy and Lou Grotta; Vivian and Martin Levin; and Linda and Donald Schlenger. In addition, Leslie Ferrin and Max Protetch were tremendously helpful with their encouragement of this project. Toni Sikes and Katie Kazan of GUILD Publishing believed in the project from the start, and my faithful volunteer here in Newark, Mimi Greef, was patient and supportive, as always.

U. Michael Schumacher of our marketing department was a brick throughout, as he handled the business side of this endeavor. Without the registrar's staff here in Newark, including Batja Bell, Rebecca Buck, Amber Woods Germano, Scott Hankins and Jason Wyatt, I could never have coped with the movement, data entry and photography of such a large number of objects. Richard Goodbody and his beautiful photographs have made each of these works come alive in a new way for me, just as Laura Lindgren has taken those photographs and designed a breathtakingly beautiful book with them. Of course, I must thank Rick Randall of The Newark Museum's Exhibitions Department for transforming this book into a beautiful exhibition. Finally, my longtime colleague and now director, Mary Sue Sweeney Price, and my deputy director, Ward L.E. Mintz, have, as always, been my cheerleaders, encouraging me to push myself and broaden my horizons.

Ulysses Grant Dietz

INDEX